GASLIGHTING

Recover From Emotional and Narcissistic Abuse

(Effective Methods and Exercises to Recognize Manipulative)

Rochell Miller

Published By Elena Holly

Rochell Miller

All Rights Reserved

Gaslighting: Recover From Emotional and Narcissistic Abuse (Effective Methods and Exercises to Recognize Manipulative)

ISBN 978-1-77485-375-7

All rights reserved. No part of this guide may be reproduced in any form without permission in writing from the publisher except in the case of brief quotations embodied in critical articles or reviews.

Legal & Disclaimer

The information contained in this book is not designed to replace or take the place of any form of medicine or professional medical advice. The information in this book has been provided for educational and entertainment purposes only.

The information contained in this book has been compiled from sources deemed reliable, and it is accurate to the best of the Author's knowledge; however, the Author cannot guarantee its accuracy and validity and cannot be held liable for any errors or omissions. Changes are periodically made to this book. You must consult your doctor or get professional medical advice before using any of the suggested remedies, techniques, or information in this book.

Upon using the information contained in this book, you agree to hold harmless the Author from and against any damages, costs, and expenses, including any legal fees potentially resulting from the application of any of the information provided by this guide. This disclaimer applies to any damages or injury caused by the use and application, whether directly or indirectly, of any advice or information presented, whether for breach of contract, tort, negligence, personal injury, criminal intent, or under any other cause of action.

You agree to accept all risks of using the information presented inside this book. You need to consult a professional medical practitioner in order to ensure you are both able and healthy enough to participate in this program.

TABLE OF CONTENTS

INTRODUCTION 1

CHAPTER 1: WHAT GASLIGHTING EFFECTS YOUR MIND 4

CHAPTER 2: NARCISSISM-GASLIGHTING 22

CHAPTER 3: TIPS TO RESOLVE GASLIGHTING RELATIONSHIPS 35

CHAPTER 4: EMPATHY AND NARCISSISM: WHAT MAKES PEOPLE WHO ARE EMOTIONALLY CONNECTED ATTRACTED TO NARCISSISTIC PARTNERS? 42

CHAPTER 5: COPING WITH GRIEF FROM BEING GASLIGHTED 51

CHAPTER 6: WHAT TO BE SURE YOU ARE NOT IN GASLIGHTING 65

CHAPTER 7: WHAT GASLIGHTING COULD IMPACT YOUR LIFE IF YOU'RE UNAWARE 77

CHAPTER 8: 100 THINGS NARCISSISTS SAY DURING GASLIGHTING 94

CHAPTER 9: THE WAY NARCISSISTS PICK AND TEST THEIR VICTIMS 108

CHAPTER 10: REBUILDING SELF-TRUST 120

CHAPTER 11: DEALING WITH THE NARCISSIST 134

CHAPTER 12: ALL ABOUT COGNITIVE DISSONANCE 148

CHAPTER 13: TECHNIQUES OF GASLIGHTING 163

CHAPTER 14: LANGUAGES NARCISSISTS USUALLY USE TO SMEAR YOU. 168

CONCLUSION... 181

Introduction

"Gaslighting" can be interpreted as a symbolic word that refers to the manipulation of mind with coercive methods. Sometimes, the perpetrator will provide inaccurate information to their victims, so that they could comprehend their thoughts in a different manner. The aim of the abuser is making their clients doubt their credibility and recall in a particular scenario. They also do not think of the victim as having committed any wrongdoing. Gaslighting is usually carried out by psychopaths people who suffer from personality disorders that are characterized by an absence of guilt towards others and an increase in antisocial behavior. These personality traits permit the abuse of others by psychopaths and they do not feel guilty or guilty. People who are normal and have tried gas light will not be convinced by it since it will reveal their facial expressions and body language. But they can also be powerful liars, manipulators and liars like psychopaths, and they do not give any clues as to the actions they take towards their victims. They aim to undermine the concept of truth in their targets, making the lies appear genuine.

The term "gaslighting" is the first time it was used in the stage production "Gas fire" in the 1930s. It was an British production that introduced gas lighting into all people. They looked into how it involved psychological manipulation , in the form of providing victims with false information to question their own memory and knowledge. The Gas Light play Gas Light finally relocated to the U.S. under the name Angel Street. Two films based on the play took place in the 1940s' early years. In 1940 there was an British production titled "Gaslight," and in 1944, there was an American film was released titled "Gaslight." Both films featured an attacker who uses an elaborate psychological trick on the victim. The perpetrator is a husband who, while gaslighting her, creates an innocent victim from his spouse. He just tries to convince her and all those around her think she's crazy. This is accomplished by using the various elements that are present in their surroundings and then insisting on the fact that his wife is wrong in her attempt to remember how the elements originally were. The term "gaslighting" originates from the scene in which the husband uses gas lamps to go through the attic of his home for treasure. After he has done this, the gas lamps throughout the other rooms begin to dim. The wife observes the lighting flickering and asks her husband what's going on however he denies it never happened. Psychologists and lay people have used gaslighting as a way to explain this kind of psychopathic behavior since the films and the play were released.

Chapter 1: What Gaslighting Effects Your Mind

Gaslighting is a dreadful thing as it can cause serious mental health problems for the person suffering. Living each day with self-doubt and confusion can be more than enough to fuel the burning flame of anxiety. As a victim of gaslighting, the perpetual feelings of self-doubt and despair can trigger depression as well. Alongside depression and anxiety It is not unusual for sufferers to develop unhealthy codependence as well as the post Traumatic Depression.

Gaslighting is a clear form of emotional abuse. Don't be frightened Don't think that just that because you know the nature of it (or that you've called your partner about it) that this is the end of this. It's not always the case. Anyone who will purposefully repeatedly make you doubt your memory and sanity is a dangerous person who won't transform overnight because you've exposed them to the wrong way to live.

Gaslighting is a shady manipulative tactic that's so effective that it can negatively affect your mind. It makes you feel very unstable and are unable to think about yourself in the way you are accustomed to. In time, this self-doubt grows so strong that you begin to turn at your abuser to find direction, clarity and direction. You're probably considering it Gaslighting isn't only something that occurs within interpersonal relationships. It is also a problem in the world of politics, by unscrupulous politicians who are determined to ensure they have the power balance to their advantage.

At first it seems like an unimportant dispute. You think there's nothing wrong with it. To be able to identify the issue for what it really is and to recognize the signs, the perpetrator is known to be of constantly lying and denying all the time the truth, even when there's evidence. They'll constantly be confusion about the subject in question, and are also prone to contradicting themselves.

The gaslighting of the mind and mental disorder

The first time that gaslighting was observed in a clinical setting was 1969. The report revealed that, in a number of instances, the sole reason that patients were in a mental institution was because somebody (or someone) was able to devise a shady plan to make them appear mentally ill. This is known as gaslighting in its pure form, where the aim is to make you appear and feel like a psychopath so that you are completely removed from the process. However, it's not always that extreme however. Most of the time people who abusers do it to gaslight in order to maintain control over you.

Sandra is an excellent employee who excels at doing what she does. But she is, for some reason, her boss is known to be always removing her from meetings. In a way, his memos don't reach her. She's tried to talk to him to discuss it however he continues to wave her off in a dismissive manner saying she's scared, and that she's likely losing the memos since she doesn't keep her factual information up to date.

Antoine is the constant subject of his dad's emotional and verbal abuse. Each time he opens out and his father encourages his son to "man up" because he's far oversensitive "like the girl."

In both scenarios it is evident that it's normal for victims to start to question their own view of reality. And with this ongoing abuse, it's just an issue of time before Sandra is convinced that she's not as sensitive as she used be and Antoine accepts his dad's assertion that he has to quit being so sensitive.

What are the effects of Gaslighting

It's an issue to discuss gaslighting or narcissists, however it's a different matter to discuss them from the viewpoint of the person you are. Let's examine the different negative consequences that gaslighting may affect your mental well-being and self-esteem. The victim has the same characteristics as a leopard who is unable to alter its spot. The most significant element in the gaslighting process isn't the abuser who is narcissistic however, but your own feelings.

In the majority of cases, when you're involved in a relationship that is narcissistic you'll be experiencing constant anxiety, unrest and stressed. You're feeling a sense despair and you're stuck in a state of feeling helpless and unable to cope. You're constantly walking around in a circle around the person you're with and you've said sorry more times than you're able to remember, asking yourself whether you're correct, doubting your own abilities, and swathed in confusion. You realize that the activities you once loved doing are no longer what makes you feel content, and no matter how you go about it you don't feel confident enough. There is that unimaginable feeling of guilt and shame that isn't the norm around your neck. It's hard to feel mentally and emotionally exhausted.

Fighting doubtful feelings. The reason that your confidence is ripped into pieces is because the person who is a narcissist starts the process from within and, over time, the doubts begin to creep into all you do. If you're trying connect with someone who's not able to be attentive or caring and asks you questions that aren't easy about you, it's natural to are compelled by asking yourself the same kinds of questions too. You believe that you're not capable of managing your own issues. In addition to adding an element of doubt You feel trapped in this relationship, which fuels your self-doubt and self-doubt.

You've probably read blogs or books, which provide the grim reality: the narcissist not going to be different. It's inside your mind, however the heart is a different matter. Similar to the narcissist you begin to believe in the fantasies of your own. "She can change her ways," your mind tells yourself but you are still stuck in the obsession they've instilled inside you. You may even be aware of when other people are being manipulated or gaslighted with their actions in their relationships, however you insist that your relationship isn't the same. You try a variety of strategies and you discover in time that you have no power. Your narcissist holds all of the cards and you cannot let go for some reason. The doubt seeps into all aspects in your daily life such as your family, career and relationships.

Feeling not good enough. It's not surprising that we've all been told that when we're soaked in sweat, blood and tears, you can get anything done. This might be true in other areas of life but not so for the Narcissist. You are thinking, "If I could only improve, they'd be able to love me like they did at first." In your heart, you realize that you'll never be good enough to impress them.

It's like they're always watching out for any slip-ups you may have regardless of the fact that the slip-ups you commit shouldn't be considered as part of an enlightened relationship. They aren't aware of the good things you do, and will quickly lay down the rules as well as make you feel guilty when you step out of the invisible, continuously moving line that is inside their minds. The more you attempt and are not acknowledged for what you did or to improve relationships with the demon and the more you begin to feel inferior and blame yourself. In extreme instances you can lose your self-identity. There is no idea of who you are. Be aware that it's not because you're not enough. You're. You're being a victim of a narcissist. an endless abyss that is never filled regardless of how much of your heart you offer.

In a sea of confusion. Today you're at the center of focus. They shower you with sweet messages, gifts, praises and belly rubs and all the nice stuff. The next day, they're far and cold. They vanish without making contact. They wander off doing whatever they like and you've got no clue as to where they are, or with whom they're. It's as if they don't even exist. If it's good it's fantastic. If it's not the case, it's not. In addition, the situation keeps changing from bad to good and back again between both of you. Naturally, all this makes you feel very uncertain regarding how you and your relationship are at! It's not your responsibility. Your narcissistic partner is extremely inconsistent. It's just the nature of the beast.

It wouldn't be as confusing If they'd been distant and cold right from the beginning. You could have had the ability to get away and go before there was a serious issue between you and them. But the person you are with can make you feel as if they understand the true essence of you. You feel as if your souls are interconnected. They let you feel this way by telling you that they're the most wonderful thing that could ever happen to them. However, they'll try to keep you from their friends who are in their lives and will not even bother to appear for you when it actually matters.

The reason you are confused is because an abuser is a devoid person who's focus is at what they consider to be the most fascinating or valuable at the moment. If that includes lavishing you with sweet things and gifts, they'll do it. If they discover something else that's more appealing, they're gone. You're basically a target for the Narcissist. You're just an item to them. If they claim they like your, they're not necessarily you they are referring to, but how they feel. Whatever "love" expressed goes away when they discover something that make them happy. If that isn't enough and boring, they're off to find something else. The only reason that you are sure that the gaslighter is in love with you is that they've got charisma and charm for days and more than enough to allow you to create something out of their sweet little grins.

The constant stream of apology. Alongside the self-doubt which affects your mind is the constant apology in spite of the fact that you do not need to or shouldn't. It is best to only apologize for a mistake. Also, you can use the word "sorry" when you observe that something else caused someone sad or unhappy to show sympathy. For example, you could tell them, "I'm sorry for your loss." It's not really the fault of you, it simply makes it clear to the person who you care about their loss.

If you're facing a gaslighter you'll discover the phrase "I'm sorry" is now your new favorite. It's not difficult for you to let them down because they're so entitled and want to keep people in the loop. You'll start to apologize for everything driven by doubts. You chant endlessly, "I'm sorry... I'm sorry ..." because you've realized that regardless of how you act you'll never be able to provide your partner the exact thing they desire.

Anxiety, sadness depression and anxiety. You're not only stressed and depressed because of the lack of support you feel in the relationship, but you feel this way too because the gaslighter isn't one who will share your feelings. You're always depressed and sad You're not engaging in activities you previously enjoyed and you're constantly feeling guilt, feeling worthless and frequently withdraw from any social activities. It's hard for you to fall asleep, and you begin to develop bad eating habits, too. In this state of depression you're not able to cope with the gaslighting effectively. Your soul is broken by this point.

Gaslighting can also cause severe anxiety. If you feel as if you are unable to resolve your relationship or return it to normal regardless of how you try the anxiety increases and eventually, it can escalate into complete anxiety. Your heart is racing. You're not breathing properly. You get dizzy spells. You're overwhelmed by the thought that something awful is likely to happen very soon.

Fortunately, both anxiety as well as depression can be managed. All you need to do is visit an experienced psychotherapist who will assist you in overcoming the issues emotions, offer the tools you need to overcome the gaslighting and abuse, and provide you with the necessary medications to improve your condition.

Learning to be helpless. As time passes and when you've been left with no choice but to endure persistent situations you'd rather avoid, you realize that you're in a position of being unable, and even unwilling to act on your situation -- even when you've got the ability to end it. This is referred to as "learned powerlessness" and was created through the University of Pennsylvania's Martin Seligman. It is learned that there's nothing you can do to address the issue, and you continue to accept it. Even when you have the chance to overcome the situation or put a stop on it do not. It's not your responsibility. You've been instructed by the gaslighter that you should feel powerless.

Gaslighting can cause helplessness, which increases your chances of having to be depressed and feel depression and. If you've been the subject of being gaslighted for a long time and you accept the fact that things will be forever. You become passive about your life, not bothering to confront your abusive partner. You are aware that you have the option of walking away but since you've been taught to keep things in order that they will improve and better, you remain. You believe that if you do your best and do your best, you will be able to achieve a better outcome for you and your partner.

The loss of enjoyment. One thing that is common for those who are victims of gaslighters is the complete lack of enjoyment in things which normally bring them joy. Perhaps you've noticed that, ever since things started to go downhill in your abusive relationship you don't want to be with those you love to be with and you're no longer interested about that Taekwondo lesson you loved so much. The world shifts between black and white and you no longer feel the need to pursue anything any more. If you could summarise your feelings and experience, it could be only two words What's the point? Due to the discontent you experience in your relationships, you are unable to anymore enjoy the simple pleasures of life. The discontent bleeds from the relationship to different aspects that you live, so simply quit caring.

Awe-inspiring shame. The worst part of shame is that it makes you make worse decisions. The person who is a gaslighter simply doesn't have the capacity to confront the guilt that they carry inside, which leads them to make the worst decisions. If you attempt to make the person accountable, they'll react by screaming and then doing something even more destructive. What effect does this have on you?

It's when you've done something that you ought to not be embarrassed about. However, you accept it, learn from the experience and move on vowing to never repeat the same embarrassing behavior again. In other instances you may choose to shut yourself off from others to avoid being judged or because fear of being judged is taking over your life. It's similar to talking about how healthy your choices for food are when you realize that you sneaked out to the store at 2 am to purchase chocolaty bars (which you consumed in private obviously!)

In the time you've been with the person who is a gaslighter, you begin to feel embarrassed as family and friends start to make a point that the way in which the way they treat you in a way that is unacceptable. It's possible that you feel ashamed of how you're treated and even if you're aware but for some reason you continue to let it happen. It's also a shame that you think that people are judging your decision to stay instead of continuing to live your life. The shame afflicts you from a variety of different angles. When you realize it you're trying to avoid contact with those who could help you get out. You get tired of telling people to make it appear that everything is in order between you and the snoozing partner. When you are able to isolate yourself from those who have your best interests in mind and you realize that you are more vulnerable to being gaslighted in the way they would like to do.

Mental and emotional exhaustion. Being involved in a relationship with people who make you feel like you're gaslighting them is exhausting. You aren't sure what's happening and you use up an enormous amount of energy trying to figure out what's going on with the person who says they love you. You're exhausted emotionally because every day (even every hour) presents a new challenge. You're going through endless arguments. You're having same arguments over and over again. There's nothing new regardless of how sincere they seem when they say they'll strive to be better.

The exhaustion suffocates your cognitive abilities, resulting in your performance in workplace or school isn't as good as it used to be. It can affect the effectiveness of your relationships , and can lead you further into isolation. The mental dangers of gaslighting are extremely real and can be very damaging to your personal life in all ways.

Chapter 2: Narcissism-Gaslighting

The gaslighting doesn't only take place in relationships with family and friends, but also in professional relationships as well as relationships with other people in the community. Additionally, we have analyzed the issue, and will examine it further, how narcissists utilize gaslighting to manipulate others and the best way to avoid manipulative behavior from a narcissist.

It is important to stress that gaslighting could harm the psychological well-being of a victim as well as their emotional health. It is therefore well for narcissists since they are able to manipulate another person in unimaginable ways. If you're dealing with someone who is a narcissist or were raised by an atypical parent You may have been the victim of "gaslighting." It's an act of verbal as well as mental abuse that is incredibly cruel, with the aim of making someone doubtful about their own mental morality. It can cause anxiety and cause you to doubt the reality of your memory or your perception of reality.

Narcissism can be described as a more shameful version that is a less shameful variant of Narcissistic Personality Disorder. Narcissism involves arrogance, narrow-mindedness and a switch in thinking processes and vanity. Other character traits that are related include psychopathy and cunning. Narcissists generally possess a high degree of confidence. But, as you can imagine it isn't just something extremely rare. People who have high to low confidence tend to be non-assuming, but narcissists typically aren't. There was a time when it was thought that narcissists possess good confidence on the surface, but in the real world they're not trustworthy. Narcissists who are genuine do not bear the burden for their own sloppy behaviour. It is typical for them to blame other people and then blame the fault of someone else. They employ a combination of reluctance, assertion as well as deceit to cause you to lose your credibility. You may decide to leave the thought of whether it's just your mind's creative side or, on the off possibility that you're confused and it's your fault.

9 Things People Don't Know You're Doing because of that you've been abused by Narcissists

1. Always questioning your self-esteem.

When you used to be confident and confident, you're now in a human pleasing state. Your family members observe that you're constantly nervous, and pondering your abilities and interactions. You're always judging yourself, deflecting compliments, or avoiding the chance to shine. You are constantly focusing on whether you're admirable, attractive and attractive enough. Then you begin to wonder whether you're toxic and oppressive once you respond to abuse (all things taken into consideration, narcissists tend to predict their own behaviour and referring to us to safeguard themselves). You start to think that you're the cause while being treated in an awful manner. Self-faults are common after abuse, but it's created by the effects of harm, not the reality.

2. Examining your ability to decide on the right choices or to see the truth clearly.

Narcissists are masters of manipulating our lives and inviting us to join their world (increasingly like the Dungeon) of deceits, bends and deliberately deceit. When you've been misled for so long into believing that the situation you're experiencing isn't true, you start to doubt whether you're viewing your reality in a way that is effective. You reconsider your options and experience a huge amount of conflict over making the right decision for you in contrast to what you've been trained to achieve to please the person who is a narcissist. It's a time to develop a feeling of a subjective discord (clashing thoughts and feelings) about the negative relationship along with other major aspects in your personal life.

3. Pursuing harmful individuals.

The more savage aspects a narcissistic companion introduces into you, the more probable you'll drift toward those who subject you to preliminaries of a similar nature. This is due to the fact it's been subconsciously subjected to strict conduct in another aspect of your life. In this way, you could have a misguided understanding of what a good behavior really means. Instead of searching for positive alternatives, victims of abuse by narcissists try to "look for an escape route" but end up encountering many more people who are toxic. This can further aggravate the harm you've suffered. It could be an indication of oneself disproving the beliefs that the narcissist taught us to believe in. It perpetuates the loop. When we are feeling alone and abandoned the feeling of being abandoned, we're less likely acknowledge that we deserve higher standards.

4. Self-disrupting.

Narcissists encourage you to doubt yourself. They cause you to suffer a brutal assault, unforgiving slurs without causing any harm, and then attack you with unresolved imperfections, fake flaws and a focus on your flaws. In doing so, they commit murder in secret using unclean hands. You're so stunned by their brutality that you are afflicted with the negative consequences of stress about your capabilities and abilities, the range of your capabilities and even your undeniable abilities.

5. Achieving others' satisfaction and being perfect.

When the narcissist would reprimand you, they sowed seeds of self-doubt that blossomed into flaws and weaknesses following the breakup. You tried everything to please your abuser, hoping to get their approval, and even get a moment of peace out of their crazed making. Therefore, it's not a surprise that once the relationship is been over, the idea of trying to please people continued to be. Human satisfaction and hairsplitting are both endurance mechanisms that operate with the idea of trying to avoid all kinds of violence (be it emotional or physical). As long as the person who abused you believed in your feelings (even just for a short time) and you were able to feel at peace. The goal is to become the witness of your perfectistic tendencies, just like your desire to be human-satisfying. Instead of making a choice regarding these inclinations, take time to observe your thoughts and feelings when you're being attracted to do something that's not true to the person you really are.

Think about, "For what reason am I really doing this? What are the issues I'm supposed to do?" Review the roots of every urge as it manifests, and choose a more beneficial option that is compatible with the things you really need and what you would like to achieve. To get rid of unnecessary stress begin to feel self-assured and be proud of yourself. When you've done something that's impressive you should give yourself a positive acclaim instead of waiting for someone else to accredit it. The habit of a person can be difficult to overcome, but new ones can emerge to take over the ones that are dangerous.

6. Removing yourself from the crowd and keeping yourself to yourself.

Abusers divide you and you begin to segregate yourself and others. Narcissists are so charming and charming that they appear to be rational ones, while inciting their victims to become out of control. In the absence of assistance from other people and you start to feel like you don't have anyone there to assist you. Your body, mind, and soul are reeling from the accident and trying to deal with the trauma.

While a period of hibernation can be expected following abuse and is, in some cases really necessary to begin the healing process Don't be apathetic about experts or people who understand what you're going through. Get in touch with the people who can help you, people who have experienced it, and those who understand the full extent of what narcissistic mistreatment can feel like.

7. Falling into misuse amnesia.

If the narcissist reveals the fact that they don't like you, you'll start to fantasize about the relationship. When the narcissist exhibits great behavior, you'll be enticed to enter "misuse memory" as a means of adapting and prove that they were excellent and trustworthy partners right since the start. It is possible to fall victim of their "hovering" attempts to lure you back into the sour relationship. To prevent amnesia, it's vital to record a list of the traumatic events you experienced with this particular person. This will help you be aware of the reality of the abuse and will help you remain focused on what you went through. The trust you place in a professional and a reliable partner can also increase social responsibility. If you find yourself rationalizing the mistreatment and then blaming the victim, they'll assist you in refocusing and aid you in remembering the experience you experienced.

8. Secure your abuser. The mistreatment of a victim can cause us to get attached to the victim. It's like Stockholm Syndrome; we were trapped in our own internal "prisoner" by the predator, and have figured how to keep them safe by securing them, protecting them, and taking their needs into consideration so as to live with. This is why people who have suffered from Stockholm Syndrome often feel pressured to talk about how positive the relationship was regardless of whether they're not in their own view. This is another reason why the overcomers of narcissists aren't able to speak straight to their loved ones regarding the treatment they received; they worry the possibility of going overboard or being too sensitive or imagining scenarios, similar to what the abuser had said they were. When you are free from the narcissist's grip, you could be inclined to protect the situation of the abuser in the interest of your own safety. It can be done from a variety of angles, from the most serious and minor. It is possible to not cooperate with the law's

requirements for exposing the subtleties of abuse or get angry with your family and friends when they are open about the problem in the context of what it is. You could not be able to ensure your security regardless of whether or not the narcissist is harassing or threatening you, fueled by a fear of being retaliated against, similar to the false impression of loyalty you gave with the narcissist throughout the relationship. If you are fighting the urge to protect the abuser, be aware that the abuser has did not guarantee that you were secure. They did not shield you from the pain they caused you or the negative consequences that followed it. The only thing you have to do following the dissolution of an abusive relationship is to protect yourself, first and foremost.

9. A distorted sense of the limitations.

One of the consequences of being manipulated is that our boundaries are becoming extremely flexible. We're now more compelled to say "yes" to the things we must urgently say "no" in order to.

We've lost our sense of authority and office in our lives, and it puts aside an effort to re-establish our limits and restore our power. It recalls your basic human rights when you've been ignored. They include the right to say no and the right to confront against indecent conduct or abuse, as well as the freedom to express anger and express it without injuring yourself. It is also possible to create an inventory of your most physical and emotional boundaries you set for the future with any connection or family kinship. They can be modified to meet your preferences and could include restrictions like "I do not tolerate anyone who is trying to fool my beliefs" and "I don't respond to ultimatums or threats."

Learn how to practice your new limits , and then finish your practice. If an intruder is trying to take you down ensure that you defend yourself in the best way you are able to regardless of whether it is just a matter of leaving the organization. Being confident doesn't always need a great signal, it's just the ability to manage your safety and security. When someone else tries to sabotage you, take the initiative to get the perpetrators out, regardless of whether it's in a tolerant but clear manner. Consider whether you're making plans to please someone else or if you really need to accomplish it. It's a process that requires practice, but you'll eventually reach your goal. Whatever you're struggling with right now you can regain your life and capacity after being victimized by the narcissist. In reality, you are able to thrive.

Chapter 3: Tips to Resolve Gaslighting Relationships

Here are some things you should do when you're studying about gaslighting. When you feel like you're being gaslighted, and you're in the middle of a relationship which makes you feel like a maniac.

Write things down.

It is time to begin writing things down. You should begin recording every conversation you have with that person, regardless of whether it's your violent Ex or spouse. Record every conversation was had, so that when he claims that you didn't have any talks with him, then you are able to contest him by recording the conversations that you have made. He'll tell you that the conversation was never held which means that you cannot be able to tell anyone concerning the exchange. Therefore, it's going to be difficult to establish a clear orientation for yourself with the reality of what it is.

Then it shakes you inside, making you feel like you're going to fall apart and suffer an emotional breakdown. If you're involved in this kind of relationship, you must begin writing every detail down, including what the food you have eaten. Since if someone asks a psychopath if you consume food that was in the freezer, they'll claim no even if they are the only person in a position to consume the food, they'll affirm that they didn't have it.

These lies will continue to interfere your reality. You must start recording everything down. It is important to note down the exact date and time. You must write down the clothes he was wearing, or which clothes the woman was wearing. It is important to record the context of the details. Additionally, you should attempt to have some small conversations. Avoid having long conversations since they're difficult to recall. If you're speaking to someone you suspect is gas-lighting, you should use shorter sentences since they are easier to remember. If you're dealing with someone who is gaslighting, you should try to keep the conversation to a minimum. If you are able to record what you would like to convey to someone, take advantage of it.

If, for instance, you suspect that someone has stolen funds from your account or stole money from your bank account , and is not willing to admit that, they're the only one with your PIN. When you're preparing yourself to approach the person and ask him whether he stole the money from your account , and you notice that there was a missing $1000 from the account, note down the exact words you'll use to address that person. Do it!

For instance, you could write "on Monday, at 12 noon, I'm going to message him or call her and inform her that he stole money from my account". No matter what they say, regardless of what they say, or whatever you do is, try to think of yourself as wearing a mental condom and being observant of every detail. Whatever the person says or what she says, attempt to note everything down in writing down what you have observed. Go to the bank , if you can , and speak with the bank's manager to find out what other possibility for what happened. The facts will help make sense of the situation. Try to keep a record of every single moment you experience for yourself, but only take it as a personal advantage.

Don't tell someone who is violent that you're recording them because they may turn violent. Be sure to contact a safe person. Find a support group for narcissists or a suspected narcissist of support group in your region in order to join them. Additionally, locate people who you can talk to in a safe manner about the issues you are experiencing. Note down each time you were gaslighted. Then, try to review your relationships and figure out a way to end the unpleasant experience since gaslighting is considered a crime. If someone walks into your home and steals your watch, and the person is breaking the laws, then you need to admit that they stole from you. If you have someone break into your home and steals your property, it's an offense.

Do yourself a favor and take some time to relax

Gaslighting is just a method of manipulating. It is a mental fact. it's as if you are inside someone's head, and they are enticed by your brain. Gaslighting can be compared to carbon monoxide because and you're not aware that it's happening to you however, he's doing it and is trying to convince the victim of their innocence. you can come out of a narcissistic abuse relationship for a year, you are able to take a look back and think about what went on. If you're trapped in the middle of a storm and you aren't aware of how large the storm is, and you aren't sure exactly where it is. you're just caught between a storm and when it takes you away you can gaze at the sky and realize you were in the path of a huge tornado.

Try to allow yourself some space from a relationship that is abusive so that you have a new perspective and a new perspective to be in a position to see the relationship. It is also important to realize that you will receive more from you once you've left the abusive relationships. It is important to begin looking at your relationship from a different angle and then begin to gain your personal immortal mind to ensure that your brain can get aligned so that you're able be able to absorb information from outside sources in a healthy manner and send it to your body in all way. When you begin to think about the lies you employed at first it could be daunting. You'll also need admit that you need help and you're being lonely.

The truth is that narcissists and psychopaths who annoy others are extremely clever. They're very smart, particularly Psychopathic people. They know what they're doing, and in the majority of cases, when you've been exiled from an arrangement, you have to be grateful for the blessings of your stars. In some cases, you'll be able heal yourself. Once you've been released from relationship, all you need to do is avoid a relationship for a time and then work to move on to the path to recovery. Learn about gaslighting, the narcissist, and learn about attachment, co-dependency and trauma and how your brain reacts to trauma. It's it not the fault of you that you been a victim gaslighting.

Chapter 4: Empathy and Narcissism: What Makes People who are emotionally connected attracted to narcissistic Partners?

What is the reason that people who are empathic drawn to Narcissists (and angry characters after all is said and done) that they aren't able to discern?

Empaths are attracted by narcissists and the majority of impulsive characters because of the fact that in contrast against the norms of the population, they are at one with their feelings. They are able to sense and feel them directly and at the exact time that the other person is trying to them.

Empaths can identify themselves with the pain of another and, in regard to the fundamental sympathy they know how to feel that pain or satisfaction. They observe and are able to discern the entire real-ness of the other. They possess a special attraction to love that is unambiguous.

Empaths are fascinated by love and the ability to connect with each other, even in the circumstance, even when one isn't content to be a part of the same.

Empaths are able to see the gap, that hurt and the distress that comes with an absence of significant affection and are convinced by their strong vision and positive thoughts that adoration will heal every broken and that their love will compensate the huge gap in enthusiasm and the confidence level of the narcissist, or the person who is impulsive after all is said and completed.

What empaths do not know regardless the Narcissist or depressed youthful person is in relationships (steady or less) in order to achieve the intention of developing vitality and not having any other motives; therefore the first step is to wear an ideal cover of affection before entering the relationship. Once the stage of success is over and they are "very silently," starting to deny themselves , and refuse to give even the slightest consideration that is normal in a couple of or three relationships.

The intention of truly young and weak people is to be acknowledged by others, and get the opinions, and to be given those that, without doubt, are not considered in youth, and which empathy is a feeling of obligation to provide.

To win in this regard Narcissists deceive the empathic, claiming that they cannot offer in this relationship, and less so in light because they do not have a limitation, but because the empath is not acting properly.

Narcissists force their victim to remain regretful, in order to increase their levels of passion execution "you should be giving me more, and later will, when I am able to show what I am entitled to I'll pay you back and continue exactly as I did towards the beginning in the beginning of our relationship. '

What can narcissists do to make their emotional partner codependent?

The initial phase of conduct that is ideal for the narcissist is through the means that the neurotic dependence is communicated through the empath in the belief that it's one of the most significant types of intense reimbursement.

The narcissist's truth and their fascination reflect, will present to the empathic the most positive image they can imagine of themselves and also the empath is usually the one who is able to survive confidence based on acknowledging their traits on the other hand (looking for an endorsement) The empath will get caught up in accepting that "just in one's eyes, as a narcissist will they consider themselves to be charming and worthy of respect and respect."

Following this passionate and fundamental extortion which authorizes the association the empath, who is usually unsure and is suffering from young deserting injuries, can be deceived into thinking they will get the pleasure and gratitude of their accomplice in the event they are more generous.

Therefore, they will in general give up, and become a part of the otherside, to tackle their issues . They'll find themselves in a state of codependence, just as they were as children with an emotionally distant and missing parent who, as hard as they tried, didn't consider their child worthy of any kind of love.

The narcissist, in fact, convinces the listener they are unique and only they is able to experience the heavenly feelings.

What is the reason that empaths and narcissists have something in the same?

"In an eloquent way Narcissists know human weaknesses well because they were children and needed to be taught the ability to stand up for themselves and to be focused on the illusion that they are invulnerable that they do not have a actual need to highlight the weak point of self-esteem in the empathic to create their desire to attain the false self that is not there and which the empathic has not asked for and which is nothing more than a projection of the false self of the narcissist on the other, a narcissistic desire to alter the 'empathic' into a rough version of them. "

The people who are extremely uninterested and temperamental are looking for an ongoing flexibility of enthusiasm and care, without sacrificing anything to compensate for their passions and emotional lapses by more evident financial and formal access in their relationship.

Once the dependency is established then the empath will be determined to make the other happy. They will be constantly committed to act in a way that will bring them joy, and not to cause them to be upset or relieve them of tasks that usually annoy them and even ruin their own lives.

The empathic must provide the narcissist with a better life than they have or to achieve their height.

The non-involved, forceful methods with which narcissists were able to avoid accepting responsibility for their actions, is a distinct section, however generally speaking the narcissists are covered by this enchantment recipe: " on the off possibility that you force me to do something that I'm not interested in or don't like, I'll make you gag and will ruin your day or be so serious that, believe me ... you'll never bother me anymore ".

A connection between an arcissist an empathic partner last?

... They as well as empaths therefore engage in relationships in the exact same "narcissistic" motive that is to affirm their worth and fill in their emotional gap. Empaths attempt to achieve this by denying themselves, living in and with the other and expecting unending gratitude , whereas the narcissist does this by making themselves a living and feeding off the other with no regard for taking or giving in exchange, due to the fact that they have a

Value must be assured through the continuous confirmation that they do not have any duties, other than the existing".

The relationship will have its own relationship until the empathic person has exhausted all their energy in the massive effort required to satisfy the accomplice. They attempts to recover the solidarity of their own circle. At that point the narcissist may begin to strain, since they are at risk of losing their ability.

The main negative effect of narcissism can be the constant, unchanging condition in which there is UNBEATABILITY AND NOIA so that even God could not generally be a supporter which is the reason why empathic accomplices frequently appear as holy or as a conciliatory victim within the network without a contact.

When empaths attempt to explain their requirements, narcissists prefer to ignore or try to confuse each other, telling them that their arguments are not justified and their demands are childish and outrageous. The empath now feels angry by the belief that they aren't worthy of love and that the judgment is never going to end since they realize that it's the other person who is owed an not worthy feeling of admiration because they've done less, and aren't able to give and having genuine feelings of inclination and confidence in an individual or a thing.

The empathic person must be taught the how to deal with the hard cost of with someone does not guarantee respect and affection; everyone is able to express their real intentions and not everyone enjoys the same level of high-pitched development. Narcissists might experience remarkable growth and a remarkable growth in these relationships, but occasionally, they are unsure of themselves, and would like to shift the burden of a possible failure completely to the other and move on to the next accomplice.

Chapter 5: Coping with Grief from Being Gaslighted

There is no reason to overlook the fact that leaving someone can cause feelings of loss. This is a crucial and healthy aspect in the whole process. Reality is the result of the person who created it, therefore naturally it's incredibly difficult to rebuild your life and let them go. If you ignore the loss, it is to fall back into the slumber of being gaslighted. Don't let that occur by not acknowledging your grief. Grief isn't just a normal thing but it is crucial for your achievement. You have been altered by the person who made it. It will require some effort to heal those wounds, and also give up the advantages it has brought you. It is not necessary to deny that there are going to be things that you should not miss. Also, you must admit that what you're grieving is the idea that your abuser might be. You may be reminiscing about and mourning the positive aspects that you shared with your partner. You're putting aside the abuse since you are in the midst of grief. You must remind yourself that you're mourning the thought of this person. The person that you are so firmly dependent on, doesn't exist. It was an alternative reality for the person just as they created an alternate reality to your everyday life. If you are able to remember this it will be easier to deal with your sorrow and look towards the future.

A Grieving Process and managing the Cycle Before we begin to explore your grief, it has to be noted that grief is cycle-like. It is not a process with any "start" or the "end" that can be measured accurately. This means that it's difficult to determine the path towards that goal however, you must not quit. Failures are inevitable and are part of life. Don't be a slave to needing to start again regardless of the number of times that it might be. If you are adamant enough about yourself to do it again and again and again, you will cherish yourself to the end of the tunnel.

You've probably heard of grieving stages. This is the reason this section will break down the phases. Every stage is described in detail, and will be followed by the steps to do when you're in the particular stage. It is possible that you will not be able to make the process quicker or simpler by employing these methods however you may be better able to make the process more productive and make it "stick," so you are less likely to begin again.

Denial/Numbness

The stage is self-explanatory but it's actually an extremely hazardous areas to be in emotionally. You're denying that it is over , and you are shut down to truly think about what's next. It is possible that you are also denying the fact that you were victimized. You might even be inclined to forget your abuser and then go back to them. You'll be tempted to defend your abuser with the words you use and do. The top of your thoughts will be all the "good moments" you shared during your time together. This is a big chance to sway your view in favor of your abusive partner. It could also mean that you are denying the reality that you had previously believed was not real. Now you are in an entirely new reality and one that is will be governed by you. While it may sound strange it is a sense of comfort that comes from knowing that the other person is in charge and there's no pressure on you. There is a lot of pressure is on you as well as that overwhelming sensation may result in feeling of numbness and denial.

Moving Through Numbness/Denial

This is an important factor to reach out to your trusted friends and family members to help you through your emotional turmoil. It is important to depend on them for a variety of reasons. For one, they will offer a view that isn't biased towards the abuser's side. Then, they will help you remember the limits and expectations you've set for yourself prior to returning to your abusive partner. They are also the primary source of accountability during this process , especially when you're close to committing a crime. They may help you remember the strategies you had made to heal yourself as well as remind you to look over your journal and discover the real nature of your relationship as well as remind you of the fact that self-care will help you to break through the unhelpful thoughts filling your thoughts and shutting you down.

Anger/Frustration

This is a dangerous stage, not because it can bring you back towards your abuser, but rather because it can cause you to direct your anger towards yourself. There could be some voice in your head which is telling yourself "This was your responsibility. I'm stunned that you got caught up in this deceit. You ought to have been aware. What is the reason you're so pathetic? How could you not have seen this coming? You're such a total disappointmentand everyone else knows it. Aren't your feelings hurting?" This, unfortunately is not unusual. As you may or may not you've become accustomed to being abused and being the victim. It shouldn't be itching to discover that you can try to victimize yourself by engaging in these self-defeating internal dialogs. If you're fortunate, this phase can see you expressing huge quantities of anger that is righteous towards your abusive partner. But, it can be a risk. There is a chance that you'll be compelled to speak up against your abusive partner in a certain manner. The kind of confrontation might sound like a way to release stress but, in actuality you are putting yourself right back into contact with your victim. This is not a wise decision for you, and it could be a real risk to you emotionally, physically as well as mentally.

Work through anger/frustration

In general, this phase is beneficial since you will be able to unleash the months, days and years of bottled-up emotions about the abuse you've endured. It is not difficult to see the ability of anger to drive you to heal. But, there are a few guidelines to ensure you are in the right direction to use your anger to benefit others instead of self-destructing. If you're having difficulty redirecting your anger towards yourself, it's time take a look at some self-care routines. You must contact your family and friends to help you realize that the person who is abused is the one who is the victim and that putting yourself in the position of victimization will allow the abuser to take the lead, once more. Also, you should refer to Chapter 8 extensively, which contains a wealth of information on how to the art of loving yourself once more. If you are angry towards your abuser, redirect that anger towards constructive actions that ensure your strength during other phases of grieving. Increase the boundaries you've already established. Make use of your anger to force yourself to do something different or to take back a piece of yourself you put aside in your relationship. Don't be afraid to let your feelings out to the members of your support group. They're there for you and being is a good way to prevent it from escalating into reckless choices. If you feel it's an appropriate and essential part of your grief and anger to confront your victim, there are methods to go about it that are more secure. Naturally, every subsequent interaction with your abuser will put you in danger. One option is to send a letter. You don't have to provide the return address, and it is safe for privacy and security. You also have the option to write, rewrite and alter what you want to say until it's the best quality is possible. It's difficult to reflect on the only time you spoke to someone after leaving and realize that you could have said something different or even added one thought. A letter provides you with the chance to think it through. Another option, which is a possible alternative is to talk with your abuser not in public space and have a friend be with you. Set up boundaries with your companion before you enter and make room for them to leave prior to you. After you leave, you should take a trip to a place where you can be seen by others before returning home to make sure that your abuser doesn't follow your footsteps. This is a route that must only be considered only if it is advised by the mental health professional to aid in the recovery process. If you do it without the guidance of a professional, it could result in a disastrous outcome. Just now, you've begun to safeguard yourself, and this could be the worst time to compromise the security of that.

Sadness/Depression

This is a feeling that could result in despair. It is possible to become bored of every aspect, not just because of depression, but in addition, because your abuser probably determined what interests you might have. Finding peace after being dependent on your abuser all day long could seem like searching for something that's absent. It can also cause you to be unable to contact your family and friends. However, the stigma associated with depression is often a source of perception of social stigma. This can prevent you from utilizing the resources you've amassed in the community who are around you. You might also begin to feel that the process of self-care has no value or as if it's not effective. You may also become disinterested in taking proper care of yourself in every way physically, mentally and emotionally. If you're at this situation, finding the path out might seem difficult.

Moving through depression and sadness

The process of grieving for each person will be distinct, and obviously, every person's experience during this time will be unique. But, a bit of activism by you can make an the world of impact. Be aware that this might not be the first step in the process of grieving However, you are aware that the time is approaching. This allows you to prepare in a variety of ways. You can inform your loved ones be aware that you anticipate that this will happen. You know yourself better than anyone else, so share with them what you'd say to yourself to help you pull yourself out of the suffocating state you are in. Let them know that being sad could result in their needs likely be ignored or even neglected during this time. It's not meant to be harsh, but rather to face being aware that depressive illness can be overwhelming. It is possible to hear that you might need them to cry with you and make sure you eat your food, ensure that you get out of the bed each day, urge you to take part in your regular activities, adhere to your usual routine of hygiene and then go to work. Do this only if you trust the person you choose to work with or split the tasks according to whom you think is the most effective in each position. Depression isn't just an emotion. It's an illness of the mind. It's likely or likely that you'll require assistance from a professional in mental health. If this option is most suitable for you, be certain to read Chapter 10 thoroughly. The chapter offers advice on how to locate the most appropriate assistance to meet your specific requirements.

Bargaining Bargaining is a difficult stage to define since it's in between the two stages of intense emotions and denial. In essence, you'll be enticed for the change in order to bring you back to the situation that was created by the gaslighting of your abuser. The requests could be made towards a higher authority or to another person of authority, to someone within your network of support or to your victim. In this moment you're determined to give something up in exchange for the restoration to the way it was prior to. It is common to begin each sentence with "What is the case if I" or, "If only I." You wish that you'll be able to return to a point that was familiar to you, regardless of how terrible it was in actual reality. This is all you have learned from that point of your life, and familiarity creates ease. It is possible that you are looking to reclaim that life, regardless of the price.

Working through Bargaining

Bargaining can be difficult to conquer because your brain is cluttered. You'll be thinking about whether your bargaining strategy will help and fix the perceived issue. This is the time to tap into reflective thinking. Take note that one of your first activities, before you left the abuser was to record your thoughts about each interaction with your abusive partner. Go back through those notes and consider the abuse you endured. Consider what drove you to leave in the first instance. Remember that bargaining to return is to offer to be a slave to the abuse. You deserve more than what you're looking for. It is a mistake to settle for someone who has lied to your and to you, and who constantly fought to make you believe that you would never be able to be able to survive without them. That's not something worth trying to negotiate for. You've got a lot to enjoy now. Consider what you've gained by quitting. They may be minor things however they all make up for you living off from the victim's control. Perhaps you have made contact with a friend from the past. Perhaps you're pursuing the same interest that you left because of your abusive partner. Perhaps you're getting an offer at work or you are getting the degree you've always had in mind. Maybe you woke up from your bed this morning and slept for for five hours without even thinking about your victim. These victories will demonstrate how far you've made it.

Acceptance/Moving On

This is where you are aware that the cycle is over and you are able to restore your life. This means that you recognize that you were a victim by the abuse, but you have escaped the assault, and are now able to begin an entirely new life. This stage doesn't require any extra steps since this is the moment to be happy. Make sure to thank everyone and everything who has helped you during this process and say thank you to them for their help. By doing this, you will be able to show that you've found the ability to live a life which is based on your personal choices. It will also demonstrate that you built your own world and one that was created by you to bring you the joy you desire. The time is now to celebrate yourself.

Chapter 6: What to Be Sure You Are Not In Gaslighting

If you believe you're being gaslighted Here are some indicators to be looking for in yourself to confirm this.

1. You dwell on the flaws in your character.

One of the primary goals for the "gaslighter" is to make you feel less confident about yourself. to alter your perception of yourself, and to create a negative image.

It is possible that your thoughts are frequently directed towards yourself, as you fret about the negative aspects of your characteristics of your personality.

You might think that you're inherently unfit or damaged, and the flaws you have make you unlovable and unlovable.

The reason that a gaslighter would attempt to get you to leave is to convince you to quit them. You're probably believe that nobody else would like to be around.

2. Your self-esteem has hit rock bottom.

This is in line with the previous issue. You are so depressed about your self-esteem that you are willing to accept disdain from your abuser, and from your self.

You don't have confidence in your capabilities and don't believe in your right to happiness.

This is why you may turn down opportunities to meet people, advance in your profession or develop as an individual.

It is likely that you experience anxiety often because you're not capable of tackling even the smallest of problems.

3. You are constantly reassessing you constantly.

Did you place that milk container in your cupboard, and the cereal in the refrigerator in error? It's best to make sure.

You're not confident in your memory and your capacity to be a human being, that you constantly think you've made a mistake.

Of of course, the person performing the gaslighting intended for this to happen, because it makes it easier for you to manipulate, as they could lie, deny facts or call you crazy... And you'll believe them.

4. Sometimes, you find yourself overwhelmed.

Beyond doubting your own thoughts, you are overwhelmed by the various aspects of your everyday life.

It could be specific to specific things, or it could be an overall feeling that your faculties of mind aren't as strong as they should be.

5. It's difficult for you to make the right decisions.

It's not surprising that you're unable to make the most basic of decisions yourself.

It isn't likely that you can make the right choice the right way, and you'll always have seek out someone else for advice on what you should do.

The person you call is, in fact the gaslighter. They claim to be the answer to your issues.

In addition, it means you are much more dependent and likely to remain with them as you don't know how to complete anything without their help.

6. You apologize a lot.

You believe that if you find someone to blame most likely it's you. You apologize constantly regardless of the source of blame the issue is. Of of course, this plays in the gas lighter's favor since they're able to not take accountability for their actions being aware that you'll be apologize to them in one way or the other.

7. You feel disappointed.

You feel like others aren't happy with your character. In fact, you are depressed in yourself. This is due to your self-worth deficiency and the belief that you're flawed in various ways. You believe that you're not enough in any way. This is why you are forced to constantly apologize.

8. You're feeling disconnected from who you were once.

In your memory from the past there's an entirely different person living in your body. A completely different you. However, you don't recognise you in the new you. It's like you're completely detached from your former self since you look at what you're currently (or or rather the way you imagine you're now) and it's not the person you were before. In a way it's like looking back on someone else completely. A past life.

9. You excuse the behavior of the gaslighter.

If a person who is a gaslighter behaves badly towards you and other people, you're fast to forgive them, or defend their actions. You think you're entitled to this kind of treatment, and you will not hear a negative word about them.

10. You lie with yourself and others in order to keep from conflict.

You've gotten used to avoiding confrontations with anyone because you've grown accustomed to being beaten down and defeated. You lie to avoid even the tiniest disagreement. You accept things that you would rather say no to. You accept the wishes and demands made by others, without doubting their legitimacy. You may even violate your morals or beliefs if you are able to maintain peace.

11. It's a question of whether you're sensitive.

One of the flaws that you can spot in one is an excessively sensitive personality. You may think that you are overreacting to situations and also to the opinions of others, and this can cause a lot of the issues you have to deal with.

12. You get nervous in front of the gaslight.

When someone enters the room, you will sense your body's muscles tightening up.

It is the physical response to the psychological and emotional abuse that has occurred. It's part of the fight-flight freeze response and prepares for the possibility of more gaslighting.

13. There's a feeling that something is not right But you aren't able to put your finger on it.

In your heart, you are aware that something in your relationship with the person isn't right. But, you aren't able to see the warning signs that are obvious to others. You don't know what the issue is and aren't certain how to deal with the issues. You'll always have an underlying feeling that it could be you to blame for the current situation.

14. Feeling fuzzy or confused.

Being confused or feeling a bit fuzzy is among the most frequent signs of feeling left feeling slighted. As an example, you're speaking to your spouse, but in the middle of the conversation you start to be confused or fuzzy. You could describe how you experience to be "crazy."

If you are noticing that conversations don't seem to make sense, you're struggling to follow the thoughts of your spouse or the subject matter of the conversation shift rapidly It can be useful to schedule a time-out. It's as easy as saying, "I'm feeling a bit confused right now I'd prefer to rest for a while. I'll be back with you later to resume the place we ended."

Once you've removed yourself away from your fog note down everything that happened, including what occurred, the words spoken observed or experienced. If you're comfortable to process your thoughts and feelings verbally, make contact with an ally to talk about the events to help you more clearly understand the situation.

15. Doubting your beliefs.

A one of the more significant consequences of gaslighting is the victim starts to doubt the accuracy of her observations. You might be left thinking about whether you actually believed you saw what you saw, or what you think you heard or thought you heard. Your spouse could claim, "I didn't say that," when you're sure you did.

If you are unsure of your beliefs more frequently that you believe you do be, you should begin recording important agreements or conversations in writing. For instance, if your spouse says that you will contact a therapist within the next week, send an email to include a sentence such as of "I'm trying to follow up on my request, and we've agreed to locate the right therapist. It is my understanding that you'll call an therapist within the next week. Let me know if you are not satisfied with your understanding of our contract."

16. Outsized responses to seemingly insignificant issues.

Let's suppose you raise an matter like your spouse's failure to get something at the store while driving home. He said he'd do. You inquire about the issue or bring it up and he responds, "What's wrong with you? What's the reason you're always breath-holding my neck?"

Of course, we all tend to overreact at times. If you have such out of the ordinary reactions to normal things frequently Gaslighting could be the cause.

17. Conversations don't produce any results.

Do you have the feeling that you are in an intimate discussion with your partner but you are unable to follow the meaning behind what's being said or the conversation appears to be in a perpetual loop that never comes to the point of resolution or conclusion? The cause could be gaslighting.

If you're stuck in a conversation rut or a tense situation, inform your spouse that you're struggling to follow what he's trying say and ask him to summarize his main idea in three or four phrases. If that doesn't work then take a relationship time-out.

18. Hocus pocus, switch the point of view.

Hocus Pocus, alter the topic when you discuss the topic or issue you'd like to talk about with your spouse and he decides to change the topic. For instance, you might say "I'd like to discuss the recovery checks we have done for our families. We've agreed to conduct one check-in per week however, we've only completed one check-in in the last months." You're spouse responds, "I thought you said that you wouldn't be interested in the details about the addiction I have."

Change of subject is a standard tactic employed by the majority of people at times in relationships. If gaslighting is the issue, it occurs regularly and on a constant regular basis.

19. You are feeling like you're on the roller coaster of your relationship.

It's easy to feel as if you're in a state of denial or have trouble keeping up to date with your spouse's recurring extremes as well as lows. At one point, you're planning a lavish romantic trip, and the next moment he's screaming at you for being three minutes over.

Unpredictability is among the most effective methods to undermine the relationship and force someone else to live in a perpetual condition of stress, uncertainty and hyper-vigilance.

20. Words and actions don't correspond.

If someone's actions and words don't align the same way, it could be insane. If your spouse tells you that "I love you" but is indecently cruel, abusive or hurtful, then you're being shocked. However you may see him as kind, charming and considerate, even when you know that he's doing things that hurt the relationship. In either scenario you'll be feeling uncertain as well as confused, perhaps even mad.

If words and actions do not coincide, you can spare yourself further disappointment and pain by paying closer at the individual's behavior and actions instead of their words.

Chapter 7: What Gaslighting Could Impact Your Life If You're Unaware

Be aware that you can stay out of the snare however, there are some dangers that may occur in the event that you're not vigilant and remain with somebody who smacks you in the face and is abusive to you.

What could happen if let's look at what might occur if you continue to be a victim of gaslighters?

Memory Loss

This is one of the things that is so frightening about gaslighting. If you've experienced gaslighting after some time, you may begin to feel guilty and suffer from a lot of self-doubt that you'll begin to forget what happened. You might not even understand the reasons for it or remember the events that transpired between these times. Many people may even have an abuser accusing them of something happening but aren't able to recall what actually happened.

Sometimes, what's frightening about gaslighting is the moment you notice that over a lengthy duration, you be able to see that you aren't able to recall the exact events because your brain and reality are totally distorted. You'll realize that you aren't able to recall things that your abuser might claim you are guilty of.

Sometimes, the person who is abusing you will claim that you did something you're doing but you're not aware of them. This could cause you to question whether you really did something. It's likely that you'll realize this after you escape.

Sometime, they'll tell you that you're abusiveand explain how they've been hurt however, you're unable to remember the reasons. Sometimes, you'll try hard to remember the violence and the trauma, but you cannot.

Another method by which to lose your memory is that you can be in a state of blankness about various aspects. If you're in a gaslight it's easy to sense your reality shifts and you'll begin to feel like you're a victim of the person who is abusing you. Sometimes, after gaslighting occurs, you don't recall the entire experiences you've experienced.

It could be a defense mechanism or it's you brain trying block out every terrible thing that has occurred to you. But, you'll be unable to remember things. The memory begins to diminish smaller and smaller until it becomes difficult to recall everything.

It is possible to have very bad brain fog, too. Abusers are known to alter your perception of reality, and when they do this you don't have the ability to recall things and your brain turns into blurred due to this.

You are always feeling guilty

One way that narcissistic abusers drag your down is to make you feel guilty all the time. This isn't a typical "oh woe is it me" idea, but the other way they make you feel ashamed because you are even a part of it. Narcissistic abusers. They'll make sure you feel guilt-ridden, continuously awful, and they'll make sure that you're the person to blame.

Narcissistic abusers can throw jabs at you, telling you that you're worthless. They'll also claim that you're nothing but an unimportant piece of garbage and are never permitted to be anything else. This is the issue with numerous users. They can cause you to feel guilty, to the point that depression or suicidal thoughts begin to surface.

You start to wonder if you're actually the person to blame for everything. It's easy to believe that you're the culprit but you're not likely to be. Even when you're completely out of the situation and removed from it, sometimes even some years later it may resurface like a ghost who hasn't yet been removed from the scene.

You're embarrassed for being alive , and it's due to the fact that your abuser has lowered you to a stage that you're not sure what to do other than to believe that, hey, you're the only one responsible, and that you're worthless.

Of course, this isn't true.

Isolation from Help

This is the thing that scares me about the narcissistic abusers. Keep in mind that they'll say that you're the only one who's insane, they are not lying, that you're the only person who's right here. They'll inform you to belie them, never any other person.

In time in the presence of an abuser it's possible to develop Stockholm syndrome, in which you are aware that you have to escape, but cannot. You isolate yourself from assistance, and frequently even when you do out, you are unable to receive the help you require.

This is because you aren't able to believe in other people. They're all lying Do you remember? Your abuser will claim that and even if you've managed quit, the memory of that abuser could hang in your head.

This is why, when those who have been snubbed leave their abusers, sometimes they aren't able to trust anyone else. They don't know if ever will be able to do so and are afraid to make the move due to what their abuser has done in the past.

Self-Doubt

Self-doubt is a result of how you were treated by the gaslighters. The aim for those who light is to make someone else feel that they are worthless and their own opinions and beliefs do not matter. Sometime, people who have been gaslighted may hallucinate and occasionally, they'll perceive things that aren't to make the person who was gaslighted feel happy.

However, self-doubt goes beyond the doubt. When someone who's been constantly ostracized throughout their lives is finally let go and goes on their own, they're usually scared about what's coming next. They've lived in the shadow of their victim for so long that they don't know how they can remove themselves from the situation.

This can lead to self-doubt. It's the self-doubt as well as the doubt of what's actually out there and the doubt about their own perceptions.

It's a pity for you.

Doubt can make you question everything you do from now on. In the end, if you've been told that you're worthless throughout your entire life, you'll likely believe that every thing you do is useless. However, it's only the gaslighting that's going on inside your head.

Gaslighters enjoy doing this because they understand that if they are constantly slammed down, should you do ever leave, you'll never become yourself again, as you're afraid of being. You'll be afraid of expressing your true self as the person you are and you'll discover that should you persist with this attitude, it will only increase the severity of your situation from here from now on For many, it could be an unwise choice that can make it harder to remember who you are.

This kind of self-doubt could limit your creativity, as well as desires So, keep that in mind. There are times when you feel you ought to do something but because you've been criticized at times, you stay away from doing it. Sometimes, this kind of abuse can hinder your creative abilities, and that's why many people advise those who have been slapped to get out as fast as they have the chance to.

Social Life Problems

Gaslighting can impact how you interact with others. The perpetrator will do to do everything they can to keep the person who has been gaslighted from their peers or family. The continuous lies and claiming they're bad people will occur. Many times, people who have been gaslighted may have a hard time seeing their loved ones until years further down the line. This could occur for a long period of.

Another thing that's frightening is the possibility that the person could end up being completely isolated from others, being dependent on the abuser and the abuser alone. It could make the victim feel that they aren't worthy of loving someone, and could make them feel that they're not secure that's the most terrifying aspect about it.

Many people who have experienced gaslighting-related effects, they'll usually experience a decline in confidence too, as no one appears to be interested in their feelings or even make the effort to meet them, while in reality, they're being pushed away from these relationships.

What's more frightening is that it can last quite a while even after you've ended the relationship. People who've been criticized in the past, will not return to their old friends and relatives immediately, because of the consequences of this. There's a reason people should ensure that they seek out the assistance that they require in order to reunite with the person they have missed immediately.

Problems in Making Choices

Decision making was performed entirely by the person who was abused, but little or no input from the gaslighted. If you've ever experienced some hesitation in the making of decisions, and you have an history of abuse it's likely that you owe gaslighting to explain that.

The decision-making was left to the other person. And any time you had to make a decision they were often viewed as untrue or wrong to make. So , why would you take decisions now?

Many who have been gaslighted during the course of their lives, may question the choices they make. They also they may not be convinced that the decisions they make are right.

This could lead to anxiety disorders in several instances. You're scared of making choices because, whenever you made one you were constantly being told you were wrong. You've been abused to the point that you're not sure how to do now, which is why making decisions is extremely difficult for people who have suffered from an abuse of narcissism. Sometimes, it can seem as if a few things are difficult to determine or, at sometimes, people may have difficulty making any kind of decision.

Gaslighting can make people feel as if their emotions and feelings aren't important, and they're often forced to make a decision about which option to take from a distance. Therefore, instead of making decisions on their own, and in a manner that will empower and support you the most, they're dragged into an ocean of stress and stress. It's not pleasant for anyone suffering from this.

A Mental Health Mental Health Side

There's also the mental health aspect of the negative effects of gaslighting. We have discussed anxiety, but it's due to the confusion gaslighters make the person who is gaslit feel. The person who is gaslit frequently doesn't know what is right or wrong and therefore is scared to take action. This could be a minor event, or it can be a huge problem in their lives which needs to be addressed.

Someone who is suffering from being gaslighted may be feeling a sense of despair and self-esteem problems. It can also cause depression, and frequently those who suffer from of this can believe that life is unattainable and that their feelings do not have any significance, and they shouldn't discuss it.

Depression is a different problem, as often being to such a low level for a long time could make one feel that it's not worth it and effort.

The other is PTSD. In the end, you had to endure a traumatizing and violent situation. The stress and anger from the actions of that person are still in the background, and typically results from this.

Then, there's codependency, a condition that could arise due to this. This is because you've lived an existence in which you were this type of relationship and it makes you feel as if you need to depend on other people.

A Refusal to Express emotions

This is an important issue. It is due to the fact that those who suffer from it will always be alert and always on the lookout for manipulative elements that can be found in any circumstance. Sometimes, this leads to people not being able to trust themselvesor others too, and many say that those who suffer from this as being always in a state of alert.

They don't want to be vulnerable, and have reasons that are legitimate. The reason is that they don't wish to get injured again like that. But the issue is this is that, although it's an interesting reason, it's an issue for some as they're unable to be manipulative to the point that their the relationship will be damaged in the future, and may face difficulties keeping a relationship going due to this.

It can happen. A lot of people who suffer from this may be unable to show feelings to others, or remain unmarried for a prolonged period in order to avoid being injured and prefer to not go through the same experience over and over again.

This is a problem since they might really love some one, but the thought of being vulnerable is not something they think they'll be able to do And sometimes they'll be hesitant to actually step up and act on it They will keep everyone in a safe distance.

Many may not view this as a concern, however, when inter-personal relationships are a problem this way, it can be a disaster for the person involved.

People Are awestruck

On the flip side to the issue, some individuals are driven to prove themselves after being abused for a prolonged period of time. This is due to the fact that they've had to endure this experience for such a long time that they're unable to move on from it except to seek validation, even though they may not be doing it in the best of ways.

People-pleasing isn't the best quality to have. It could make people refusing to change their behavior because they believe it is pleasing to other people. They could be viewed as being a bit smug, and tend to want to keep their friends at bay even if that requires sacrificing a part of their own self-esteem in the process.

They are prone to doing harm to themselvesand others for the sole reason of validation. The problem is that this can open the door to abuse. Some people may not be able to sympathize with someone suffering from addiction and not everyone can understand. Certain individuals will actually use the person to advance their own goals. Some of the abusers could take it to the point of attempt to manipulate the victim to manipulate them again. From there they can become the subject of abuse by another.

The perpetrators of abuse look for victims such as this because they're vulnerable to manipulation and they'll jump right into the fray and turn this person an easy target. The person who suffers from this doesn't actually escape the abuse, instead they are the target of another abuser's assaults, regardless of whether they're similar or different.

The other side that most people aren't aware can occur if you're not cautious and you end up being stuck by the ups and downs of the. It's just the same as not expressing emotions at all, and is likely to be more severe.

This isn't even mentioning that all of these aren't issues. They are definitely problems but people aren't aware that if abuse isn't addressed or dealt with and dealt with, it's only going to get more difficult for the person being slighted to finally get over it and take action to stop the issue. It's the reason why many people have to realize that in order to make the most favorable possible situation to themselves and their family, they must to take the situation in their own hands and take action to stop it.

It's not easy to get out of However, it's possible. We'll discuss this. Recovery can be lengthy due to the fact that the abuse creates uncertainty at the beginning of it. As people grow older, they distrust everything they see and, in many cases, getting over this could be a lengthy process.

However, we'll explain how to escape and how you can utilize this book to evade the actions of your abuser and be more confident about recovering from the whole experience.

Chapter 8: 100 Things Narcissists Say during Gaslighting

If a narcissist tries to employ the gaslighting method to get you to do something, they can use many different phrases they could use. Knowing the various kinds of words they use can aid in understanding what's happening right before your eyes. Knowing is power particularly when you are dealing with a narcissist who is gaslighting you.

A lot of these words could resonate with you If you're engaged to someone who is a Narcissist. Be aware that you're not alone and are able to recover from the abuse that you've experienced or could continue to endure. Knowing that there are certain words that narcissists employ can help you combat the abuse they hurl to you regular day basis.

Here are 100 questions or phrases, as well as comments which narcissists might use while they try to sway you:

What is it that makes you insane?

Have you ever thought about the possibility of be Schizophrenic?

You are always making up stories in your head.

You should definitely seek out help.

If I believe that something isn't right I will not do it.

You are always so defensive.

You appear like as a child.

What is it that makes you appear like a child?

Communication skills of you are severely not up to scratch.

This isn't an argument. it's a debate.

I'm not trying change your life.

There is always something going on, isn't there?

You're really insane, aren't you?

I wouldn't be able to say anything negative to anyone if you did not intend to cause me to be angry.

It's clear why people aren't happy with people like.

I was thinking you were a decent person. I can realize that I was wrong about the way you're being.

Just get over it.

I'm not going to get into your games.

Your life will turn into an absolute nightmare If you decide to inform my story to others.

You're really stupid You're really dumb, aren't ya?

These kinds of responses are the reason people consider me to be the wise one in this situation.

You'll lose me If you continue this way.

I'll just go along with it to ensure that people will choose myself over the other.

Do you realize that I'm not able to beat you?

You're always making you look like a fool.

Man, I am very sorry for you.

Yes, you are higher than thou.

Oh, poor you.

Don't act like you're an innocent victim.

It's clear why I don't like you when you do this.

What is it that you are saying you mean? I'm not an attractive person Everyone else believes that I'm.

If you continue to drag me down, I'll keep my distance from you for the rest of my life.

It's a mystery to me what I consume alcohol (or use drugs depending on the circumstances).

Every time I am in my vicinity I feel like a shithole.

Are you listening to yourself? You seem like a crazy.

You're taking your previous problems out on me.

What is the meaning of trying to take control of you? This is absurd.

I will only do what is most beneficial for you.

What causes you to always have an issue?

You cannot be content You can't be happy forever, can you?

I will be missed when I'm gone, since I'm the most wonderful thing that's ever occurred to you.

I cherish the most I could ever.

Do you realize that all our issues stem from you? It's all your fault.

What is it that makes every single thing cause you to be down, or can it cause you harm?

You must find something to be unhappy about on a regular basis you know?

Do you find it enjoyable to be moody throughout the day? That must be because it's so consistent.

There is no one else who truly likes you, except me.

You dare to try to influence me.

Your kids aren't a worry to me.

It's not your fault here, everybody is with me.

You are truly insane.

Why do you seem so unmotivated?

What are you referring to? I've never said anything like that.

Stop being so sensitive.

I know exactly the thoughts you have. I can read it across your body.

Why don't you just be quiet for a second?

Remove that look from your face before I take it for you.

You're a lowlife.

You don't have any idea.

Don't be worried about anything.

You're an odd duck Aren't you?

If you continue to talk about me, you'll regret it.

There's no better person to serve you than me.

Who would want someone who is like you?

I'm so much more intelligent than commoners like you.

Aren't you able to see how significant you are? I have major projects and all you have to do is the paperwork.

Stop wasting my time with all your insanity.

You can do it the way I did or go out.

The males are more superior than the females.

I understand the reason you behave as you do; you're not balanced.

If you're willing to take a moment to listen, I'll give you the answer you've been searching for.

Wait and see what happens.

It's no wonder that your children are so messy They're as you are.

Have you ever considered if you're bipolar?

Why do you constantly refer to the past?

Why do you constantly approach me at the most inconvenient moments?

You always treat me as that there's something I'm not doing.

Everyone in your circle laughs at you from behind.

There is no one who really likes you , except for me.

There's always something wrong Isn't it?

Let me go? Okay, but you'll never be courageous enough to do that.

Are you delusional?

Who are your friends? You don't are friends with anyone.

Why would anyone want be your friend?

Man, you've certainly gained weight, haven't you?

There is no love that is as strong as the one I show you.

There is no one there who is more superior than me.

If you do leave me, I wish you luck in finding someone who will put up with you.

You won't be able to survive without me.

It is insane to think that I actually said that.

You might want to see an Psychologist.

You are the one one who would love someone similar to you.

Stop nagging me.

Geez, why don't you just be funny?

Why do you have to be so critical?

I'm sorry to bother you. I was working.

You must grow up.

Do you not see that you initiated this thread and not me?

Can't you just get over it?

What is it that makes you angry about everything?

Each of these words or remarks can be used to manipulate. They are all over the lives of those who are involved in relationships with Narcissists. These may seem like normal to say when engaged in a heated argument but when you're having a good relationship with someone who cares about you, they're unlikely to be saying the kind of things.

The harmful nature of these kinds of things is sure to affect any person. Whatever your level of intelligence are, they will affect you in the same way. When we are told repeatedly the same thing, eventually we are conditioned to believe that. Every time we hear this we feel a little less of our self-worth decreases. Thus, knowing these phrases at the beginning of a relationship or friendship can help you to avoid the negative effects they could affect the person.

It is more difficult to leave when you have to deal to a parent family member. This is particularly the case for those who live in the household of your parent. There's nothing you can do other than to understand the situation so that the impact isn't as negative. Be aware of what's happening as well as find an place to express your anger.

It is important to keep in mind that it's very unlikely that you will be able change the behavior of the person who is a narcissist.

The most important thing you can do is ensure that you are safe and understand what they're trying to do to achieve total control.

We have previously discussed the importance of mindfulness when confronted by someone who is a narcissist. This is especially true when you listen to these kinds of remarks or phrases. Take a moment to be present in the moment and look at what's going on. It is likely that what they say are not true.

They're simply trying to make you be a slave to their beliefs in order to have control over your life and the relationship you share with them. When they make you feel uneasy and making you feel bad, they will make you will make you feel good.

The narcissist is living in a distorted reality, in which everything is focused on them. They are self-centered and do not seem to take into consideration the harm their words can cause. Being aware of their methods and knowing that their words are not true will to ensure that your self-esteem doesn't plummet.

The conversation with the people you trust in your life must always be considered when facing someone who is a person who is a narcissist. You might feel that they aren't understanding or don't take note of the harm that your narcissist friend has done to you.

This isn't true. The people who have been there for you and loved you will continue to love and value you. It is likely that they're worried about you and may suggest contact with them.

Being able to have a solid support system when you're in a position that is a result of gaslighting is essential to keeping your self-esteem and your sanity. It can be very difficult to deal with when someone is putting little digs at you each day. Most people don't even begin to recognize it until it's too late, and have been afflicted by these methods for a long time.

It is crucial to remember that you shouldn't quit trusting those you have trusted prior to entering any kind of relationship with an Narcissist. They'll be able to offer new perspectives on the situation and, most likely, they'll be able to see what's taking place as it really is. If you don't be able to see it, that does not mean that it doesn't happen. Gaslighting can make it extremely difficult for those who is in the situation to remain conscious and aware of what's taking place, therefore relying on your loved ones to guide you is a great choice regardless of whether it's difficult to view it from their point of view.

If you've not been in a relationship that is narcissistic for long and you are able to recognize these types of situations and you're more likely to stop them before they do any serious harm.

Being aware of the issues you are facing is a challenge however it is feasible. The most effective decision to make once you begin to notice such comments and words pop up is to end your relationship with the person who is expressing these things to you. If this is not possible and you are unable to do so, you need to begin to reaffirm your beliefs and understanding that you are who is worthy of respect and love regardless of the vile and demeaning things being said about you.

The words and remarks we've listed are some of the top choices of those who use the gaslighting technique However, you should be aware of numerous others. Your companions, friends and family members shouldn't be talking to you in this in a snide manner. It is important to treat everyone with respect and kindness. The words we use to express ourselves have a significant impact on others and those who are truly concerned about you would not use such a sexist language in a way that's demeaning, and harmful to one's mental health. Stand to defend yourself against those who talk to you in such a way, so that you know that you are worth it and have good relationships that are worth your time.

Chapter 9: The Way Narcissists Pick and test their victims

There's no doubt that you've wondered what it would be like to become a victim of the Narcissist. You're a decent person and isn't worthy of being victimized so badly at all. What do you have that draws the person who is a narcissist? What do you have that causes them to say, "Aha, there's a perfect target to put all this crime on"?

It's not the fault of you being selected as the narcissist's mate. They happen to be the most effective and deadly kind of predators on emotional levels. They know the most effective people to choose to target, and you're certainly not a random target. They aren't targeting you because you're a bad human being, and so do not believe that you're not good enough.

Things About You That make You a target

You're a loving, caring person who's enthusiastic about helping others. In the beginning of the relationship is lovely and gorgeous. However, things change quickly. When you first begin your relationship If you're a person who gives then you'll naturally want offer more and more to your spouse. The good thing about the first few months of a relationship is that it's particularly well for narcissists, because they are your sole and only. Your focus is all always focused on them and they are awestruck by it. It's the emotional vampires they are. As time passes the narcissist will suck you dry, systematically getting power over you, without even realizing what's happening.

You've got something that the gaslighter would like. It could be your way of life. It could take the form of money, power or even power. Whatever the reason they are looking for something from you. It's likely that your relationship started with the narcissist ever-helpful. If the second aspect does not work their way, and they simply take away the carrot and you're handed the stick. Once it becomes apparent to them that they know what they're actually seeking and it's not yours and they'll only intensify the tension already present. The narcissist is only looking for one thing out of your relationship and that's total control of what they think you're doing.

It was a troubled childhood. If you've had the unfortunate experience of being raised in a dysfunctional home and it's a problem, it could make it difficult to discern the signs of abuse or your boundaries are not respected as it's all you've experienced. You may also be having trouble creating boundaries. And when you do establish boundaries, you're likely not sure regarding your boundaries. This is why the narcissist will be attracted to you. They're not fond of limits. They choose you in order to make use of your weakness to gain their own personal goals. As part of their exploitation they'll swoop into your life and take care of all the work for you. At first glance, it appears like they're extremely useful, but what's happening is that they're creating a situation in which you're unable to take care of yourself. It's easy to rely upon them to do everything. Their heroic acts of service can only take away the feeling of independence and empowerment from you.

You're compassionate and empathic with a vengeance. There is never a person who is a narcissist's problem. There is always someone or something else at fault for their mishaps in their lives, as it relates to them. When you hear their sad stories and stories, you feel intrigued, trying to help someone in some way because you're sympathetic and understanding. This can be a problem for the narcissist as they're the focus of your attention. Naturally, what started out as a noble idea on your behalf turns into an unhealthy, life-threatening relationship at the end of the day.

You continue to accept blame for something even though it's evidently not your responsibility. In your ever-growing relationship with the narcissist you'll find that they're constantly hiding or outrightly saying that you're the cause. They'll put the blame on you and then pile on the guilt too. They'll claim, "Well, if you weren't acting like you did, I wouldn't be so up in arms." Instead of focusing on the awful thing them doing to you moved blame onto you and claimed it was your fault that they did what they did at all. They'll get their feet wet to make sure that you don't be able to return to the subject that is at hand.

You're alone and in need of love. The narcissist is always looking for those who have a profound desire that must be met. They are enthralled by the fact that they have friends, or require love, and will do anything to fulfill that need. At first you may think that their enthusiasm is a positive thing. You may think it's an unadulterated passion! But that's not the situation. In time the intensity decreases and increases in intensity. The warm and affectionate Narcissist suddenly becomes warmer than the cold and distant as an uninvolved stranger. It leaves you perplexed, wondering what made a mistake and the way you could repair it so that you can return to that person who used to hold the most brilliant, hot torch for you.

It is not your fault when it comes to conflicts. If you are a regular of avoiding confrontation in order to preserve peace, then it is a perfect target for a narcissist to pursue. Most people who aren't confrontational suffer from an extremely strong anxiety about guilt loss, and even the end of relationships that are important to them. If the narcissist is ranting and you are frightened, the anxiety in you and it becomes active and can even impede the ability to think rationally. You'll do whatever you can to for peace. the more you stay away from conflict to the narcissist, the more she gets attracted to you.

What the Narcissists Tests You for

When you let the narcissist to have their way at first it's hard to realize that you're being examined. One test that you must pass! To pass, you need to stand up for yourself defend your rights and not be apprehensive or open to change.

It's it's one thing to know at some point the narcissist has testified against you or is going to test you. However, that won't help much if you don't be aware that you're being tested. Let's take a look at the "tests" that are set for us to see if we are able to be a failure, and succeed each time!

The narcissist promises you that they'll contact you by the specified day and hour, but they do not. This isn't an accident. It's an exercise. What happens when you miss that date is they eventually contact you and pretend that all is well even though you've was waiting on your call to be ringing after they told you they'd call but they didn't. Now , they're talking to your as if nothing is wrong, even though they'd never said they'd contact you when they asked to. You're now feeling like an anxious mess! What's the objective? They want to know how you react. They want to see what you will do. They'll have a plausible excuse, such as there was a sudden occurrence or they've forgotten, but it's not a mistake. They deliberately chose not call , because they wanted to know your response. If you do confront them on it, they'll claim that you're acting excessively. It's not to say that each occasion this occurs, you're dealing with someone who is a narcissist. If you criticize someone on this, they'll truly apologize, even if they did not intend to make the mistake. If you're talking to someone who is a Narcissist, they'll be angry by the fact that you've made this an enormous deal. If you know someone who is doing this, it's time to let them go because they're not worth your time or energy.

The narcissist demands that you modify your self-image or about the way you appear. If you've just met someone or have just gotten into a relationship and then your spouse wants to change something regarding the way you prefer to dress or the way you perform things. This could be a warning sign! Nobody who is in the right mindset would ever tell anyone they have just met or just began dating to alter this or their perception of them. No matter what you decide to do, you must be your own person. Don't make the mistake of thinking, "Well, this relationship will last over the long term Let me modify the way they see me." Don't do it! Do what you want to do, and If they're not a narcissist and they're perfectly happy with you just as you are.

The narcissist will often share their horrible ex-lovers and their awful childhood. It's also a test to see how you decide to react to their stories of misery. While they talk the stories, they'll also be asking you questions regarding your own childhood experiences and your own childhood. It's possible that the narcissist actually suffered abuse or suffered a rough time as a child. That's certainly an awful thing regardless of who it was that it happened to. Be alert, as they could be searching for your weaknesses as they attempt to make a mental empathy with you. They want to understand the reasons you become weak and soft; eventually, they'll be able to leverage this to gain advantage. The first encounter with someone you've met is not the ideal opportunity to discuss your past that was dark and traumatic or the trauma that you've been through. This is not a good way to start to a friendship or a relationship.

The narcissist claims, "You can trust me," when you've both only met for the first time. One thing to remember about people who can't be trusted is that they're more likely to say "You are able to trust me" even when you've just have met. They won't discuss such sensitive topics that require trust when just meeting , unless you're participating involved in group therapy or some other activity. There's a natural progression of events related to friendships and relationships. The one thing you don't want to take that assertion as factual and then open up, as you might be dealing with someone who is a narcissist. If you're open about it to them, they'll think it's simple for them to enter your head and they'll have a lot of evidence to apply against you.

Sometimes there's no reason to be

There are instances when you're the target of a narcissist. This is not because of something specifically, but because you were in the incorrect place at the right moment at the wrong time. Don't think it's because of something you're not doing since they choose to focus on you! There's a thing known as transference that narcissists are guilty of. They take their anger or rage and direct it towards the most accessible, closest and easily accessible person they are able to be bullied by... as well,, sometimes they're you!

Whatever the circumstance it is important to know that you are the only person who is yours. It's not necessary to be an abused victim. In my 30s, when I realized that I wasn't required to continue being a victim of others. Being from a dysfunctional household I didn't know which boundaries existed, or what was considered unacceptable. However, I learned this over time and, since I have been a little more peaceful and free of Narcissists. If I do come across one, I discover that I cherish my joy and freedom enough to not let them ruin my life. I'd love for you to have the same joy and freedom, too. If things have been so bad that you aren't sure you are able to break free, you must seek the help of an experienced professional counselor to help you regain your sense of self.

Chapter 10: Rebuilding Self-Trust

The majority of the information that is in this book will have you looking to other sources for the support you require. This is a crucial element of recovering from gaslighting. But, there's one person you cannot avoid when you are on the path towards a new you that is you. You were manipulated for all of your life. You were told that you were in error for a long time. You were slammed and deceived and deceived. This is the right moment to not leave those things behind, instead of replacing them with healthier practices. The most significant aspect of getting over gaslighting is feeling worthy. The person who abused you has destroyed your inner self and told you that it wasn't worthy of keeping. It's time to go back to the inner you revive it, then rebuild it. Even before you're ready to be a lover or trust another person you must first believe in yourself and love yourself. This is another way to avoid becoming a victim of gaslighting once more. You'll love yourself far enough to let it continue, or to even happen at all.

Steps to Growth

Like many of the exercises included in this book building confidence in yourself is a process. But, it's something you will be able to avoid having to go through again until you've built trust in yourself and love it again. This level of self-confidence is a point where you feel safe and secure completely. To reach that level However there are some steps to help you build your self-confidence over time. These aren't sequential steps but rather a set of ideas that you could mix-and-match according to your preferences. They can be repeated, eliminated and reimagined however you like. They are intended to reflect you. Making them yours can enhance your experience and more empowering.

1. You control your destiny. This knowledge is crucial to your development and your freedom from being gaslighted. You are in control of the way you feel and

the decisions you make. You hold the power you've never experienced before, and you're prepared to use it to your advantage. You are the master of that power. You have the right to do so. That's why you decided to leave your abusive person. Try when you say to yourself several times "I I am the one in charge." You can even go one step further and repeat that to yourself as you stare at the mirror. Repeat the phrase until you are sure of it until you feel confident or smile at yourself. You're in charge.

2. You've been neglecting yourself since you were under the guise of being gaslighted. It is now the occasion to pamper yourself. It is possible to initially be hesitant about the idea, but it's just another indication that you truly need it. You deserve an escape, some enjoyment, or a little indulgence. Set out for a date and treat yourself with delicious food and enjoyable occasions. Explore what it is like to be alone and be content. It's an incredible feeling of freedom.

3. Self-trust is only possible with honesty in your self. If you're thinking about it do you let the truth out? If not, then you're hindering yourself from growing. It doesn't mean that you have to be a victim to yourself. It's more of a problem that you're ignoring the things that can be a source of happiness for you. Be accountable to yourself, be reminded why it's crucial to make the effort. Go through your journals from the past. Are you living the lifestyle you'd like to live? If not, then take the time right now to consider ways in which you are preventing yourself from being happy.

4. When you realize that self-honesty is a virtue You need to have some self-awareness. What are you feeling? Why? Consider your emotions in a meaningful manner by journaling or meditation, praying and sharing with a close friend and so on. It is essential to tune into your emotions so that you don't forget about your needs. Release your emotions because your freedom can help you grow daily.

5. Being honest about your feelings could cause you to be in trouble areas. It's perfectly normal and healthy. Recognizing your weaknesses isn't negative. It is a way to that you are aware of areas where you should be more attentive. These are areas where you need to make use of other strengths that can counteract the weakness. There are also areas that require external assistance. Are you in need of an accountability buddy, tracking technique or even a therapy therapist? Select the one that best suits your needs to prevent your weaknesses from taking over your strengths.

6. If you are able to identify flaws, you could feel unsure that is not good in building self-confidence. This is why it is important to examine your self from the outside and identify things you love and admire. What makes you feel proud of you? What is it that makes you feel happy about yourself? Are there any peculiarities or "isms" that give you confidence in yourself? If you're struggling with this task, don't be shy to speak to someone within

your support group. Tell them the reason you are doing this so that they don't believe you're only looking for praises. Let them know that you are looking at yourself in a fresh manner, and they'll be able to see it. 7. One of the most difficult aspects of self-confidence is respect for self. Consider the situation as follows. If you wouldn't be able to say or do something to your closest friend, why would you make it happen to yourself? In the same way, if you would not allow someone to say or do something to your favorite friend without taking action Why would you be afraid of making yourself stand up for yourself? Also, you are an excellent person. Your standards must be high as you don't have time to waste with people who don't appreciate your worth as much as they ought to. Be proud of what you do, who you are, how you behave, and in the way you treat others around you.

8. Self-trust can be correlated with self-confidence. Naturally, you should not completely isolate yourself and shut off

with the rest of humanity. You'll need other people to assist you. But there are also instances when you are the one helping yourself. Make it a point to be generous yourself something, however that might mean. This could be simple as taking a day off work due to the fact that you're overwhelmed and require some space. This could be as difficult as accepting that you have relapsed in the same way as your victim. You can give yourself unconditional love. You'll be amazed at how liberating it feels to know that you might have the answers inside yourself.

9. If something goes wrong, you are responsible for the situation. If it is the result of your own decision, then that's acceptable. The most important thing than the issue is the solution that you develop. Instead of thinking about how things were wrong, you'll discover how you can fix the issue. The issue you created had to solve, which requires strength and imagination. This also means that you take responsibility for the way you live your life,

in a manner that gaslighting does not. You have the ability to own your victories and failures in equal measure.

10. Don't compare yourself with others. This can lead to an easy way to fall down a slope which you shouldn't be taking to be on in the course of your existence. Be aware that you only see the things that someone is willing to share. So even if you think they're catching up to you in any way, keep in mind that you are only seeing only the top of the hill. Everybody has challenges that they have to overcome. It's not a race to the finish line. It is not necessary to "keep up" with everyone else or imitate anyone. Selecting a role model might be a good starting point but at the end of the day, you must be your personal role model. There's no one that you can look up to or that has accomplished exactly what you've achieved.

11. It's fine for you to stand out. It is not necessary to do these exercises exactly in the manner you've been written. Your own path is entirely yours. If you don't

create something unique for yourself You run the chance of reverting to the old ways of life. Your strategy should be based on your own desires and values, as well as the things you want for yourself. Avoid getting caught up in the notion that you are "normal" as well as "acceptable." Keep in mind that you made a promise to be honest with yourself. Be open when something isn't working, and figure out an approach to help it be beneficial for yourself. Making this type of change can be a fantastic way to improve your emotional and mentally.

12. As your self-esteem grows, more so is the need to review other areas of your personal development. What values were you holding most dear prior to the beginning of this journey? Did they remain the same? Perhaps you are now looking to alter some of your limits. Perhaps you'd like to change your routine for self-care. Perhaps you've outgrown certain people you have in your life and want to make the transition to higher high-quality friends. Whatever the reason you are in, allow

yourself to seek out more friends and make changes that help you.

13. This could cause you to to take chances. This is a great indicator that you're seeking out something that is different from who you were before and after your period of abuse. There's a reason why there is a saying that says that zero risk are worth the reward. If you don't try it, you'll never know whether that chance has altered your life in the positive direction. Don't abandon any cautionary tales or compromise too in regards to limits, but don't be afraid to break beyond the confines that you have created around your self. You can be the person you'd like to be today. Revel in the knowledge that you're still growing as an individual. It's an exciting and fulfilling experience.

14. The process you take must be guided by goals. Choose the positive changes you would like to be able to see within your life. Utilize the patterns you observe in your thoughts and feelings to select areas

of growth. It could be that you wish to be less stoic. It could be that you wish to be confident in your ability to offer suggestions in the workplace whenever you are thinking of thoughts. This could mean practicing self-confidence in difficult situations. Whatever your objective it is important to accomplish two things. The first is to make it positive. Do not use the words "no," "never," and "do not." Make your goals in a positive way. Then, you must achieve your goal. It is not worth trying to forget your abuser completely or not show any evidence that you were ever victimized at all. Sure, the experience was traumatizing, but look at the things you've built over the years. Enjoy the fact that sure, abuse did occur however, you are in control of what happens in the future and how you react to it.

15. Be gentle with yourself and take your time. You are going through massive inner changes in the present. Don't expect too much from yourself that you are trying to build self-doubt instead of confidence in yourself. Every win, no matter how tiny,

will contribute to your progress in this process. Take advantage of those wins instead of getting distracted by the things you've not yet accomplished. Of course, there's plenty of growth to come however, right now you're already growing in tangible ways. This is a major transformation from the one that you lived when you felt feeling slighted. Return to the place you were at the beginning and you'll be amazed by the change in your inner conversation and the way you think of yourself. It will awaken you to the significance of each move, no matter how small.

16. Consider ways you can be a lover of yourself. "Love" is a word with many meanings however for you right now, "love" means patience compassion, forgiveness, understanding and self-care. Be sure to show yourself love regularly and do it in the form that is most meaningful for you. There's no reason to purchase something if you think gift items meaningless. Be honest with yourself and discover your own personal reasons to feel

valued. Perhaps you decide to try having a spa day in the beginning and you feel totally revitalized. You might try to give yourself positive affirmations each day prior to when you begin your day, and at the end of your day. You can lift yourself up in any manner makes sense to you.

17. There will be occasions when you fall and make huge errors. It is possible to take one step forward , and seven steps back. It's fine. Humans are human. This is part of the process as well. It is not like a child's story character that is perfect all the time. You are a real person and humans are prone to mistakes. You'll stumble, trip and even fall over several times. This is not a problem. You have to get up and continue to work. When you feel like you're not able to, remind yourself of the person who abused you and how they affected you. Utilize that as fuel to help you as you strive to achieve greater as well as better in your life. The mistakes you make can be used to grow and can show you how to avoid them for the future.

18. When you begin to build self-confidence the trust you build must be unrequited. This may seem impossible however it's not to say that you can be flawless. This is to mean that you'll believe in yourself through success and failing, regardless of results. The decision you made has negative or positive consequences is not important. It is not important. You will continue to push forward. You will continue to show you are okay to be true to what you have decided throughout the entire process, even if you acknowledge that you've have made mistakes. You require this degree of confidence. You deserve unconditional affection and encouragement from you.

Chapter 11: Dealing with The Narcissist

First, knowing can be the very first thing in breaking free and stopping the narcissist from ruining your life.

What can I do to tell whether I'm being victimized by Narcissists?

It could sound like an absurd question. People who are looking from the outside are unable to comprehend why the person who is abused is so difficult to leave the abusive person. It's not as simple as it seems. It is not always physical, and it is often delicate and difficult to recognize. The victim has to break free from the spell the narcissist is casting to see the abuse. Even if you are aware of this, it's not easy to get out. Here are a few indications that you're being victimized by the narcissist

You've lost your confidence and confidence. You're always anxious about yourself and are unable to voice your thoughts.

You no longer have or have you been in the same contact as your families members and your friends. You feel lonely from other people. I have met a survivor of domestic violence who claimed she believed that, in the event of her death there would be no one to come for her funeral.

Friends and family members have expressed concern about your current situation as well as the way you are treated.

You feel depressed or sad or anxious, and you aren't enjoying things you used to enjoy.

After a heated argument or simply having a chat with the narcissist think that what you made was stupid or wrong.

You notice that the person who is a narcissist appears to be friendly, engaging and charming with others, however, he is critical, condescending and evasive when with you.

You no longer care about your appearance or health. Personal grooming can take so many hours of effort.

If you have kids you may notice that they're in trouble too.

You are the one who is providing and doing everything possible to maintain the relationship. The narcissist is expecting to see this from you but will do nothing to assist.

You are giving all you can but not receiving love in the return.

It's hard to understand why the narcissist will keep accusing you of or accusing you of things that you'd never think of doing.

How did you enter into an intimate relationship with someone who is a person who is a narcissist?

Certain traits can lead us to be a victim of the narcissist's trap.

Empathy

The person who is narcissists is lonely, broken and empty person. The empath's compassion and love is exactly what the narcissist's looking for. The empath wrongly believes that he or she can help the person who is a narcissist. The narcissist is not fixable. He wants in breaking the spell in order to have control. The narcissist is a God complex, and when he comes across people who are willing to give up their time for a romantic relationship It's just too to resist.

Kindness

You're looking to please, and you're quick to offer praises. If someone hurts you're quick to soothe the hurt. The narcissist is aware of the source of narcissistic supply that you possess and would like to have to have that supply. It's not just because he is in love with you (although it could be a part of his bizarre notion of the word love) It's because he is seeking this supply.

Vulnerability

Even without the characteristics the narcissist likes If you're willing to allow the narcissist in your life, he'll. You may be a committed romantic or fear to be left alone. The person you were with may have tricked you into believing he could aid you financially. What ever your weaknesses are the narcissist made use of it. This is the way of the person who is a narcissist.

Credulity

While being kind and well-intentioned you were unaware that a narcissist existed. You believed in the narcissist's methods of deceit. You believed that everyone is just as lovely as you are, and the narcissist made a profit of this.

the Narcissist's Mind Games

It is important to return to the way you were misled to avoid falling into the same trap.

Love bombing

It's the typical first step to dating. He'll throw "bombs" of messages, notes during the course of the day. texts presents and chocolates, flowers, whatever it takes to get you to drop your guard and believe that he is truly in love with you. You might sense a lack of sincerity with his love bombs but you ignore it and allow yourself to be swept along with the flow. You start to attract all the attention, and you become a prime victim for his ultimate plan to manipulate and control you.

Listening

You are amazed by how great listener he can be. He seems to be attracted to you as the way he asks questions is that he appears to be writing notes during your conversation. What he's doing is collecting information and identifying the weaknesses. He's actually making notes in order to learn how to trick your mind. Listening well usually a positive quality. However, if the person seems to be excessively curious all at once, and if you are bombarded by excessive personal inquiries be aware of the alarm bells.

Mirroring

He will attempt to convince you that they are extremely similar to each other by continually the extent to which you are. The most important thing for the narcissist is to entice you. Therefore, he'll be adamant about every word you make up, laugh at your jokes, and claim to have the same taste in food books, movies, and other things- everything to entice you.

The treatment is silent

This is another form of punishment to punish a perceived offence. The narcissist may do this over a period of time, without any explanation, to slap you. This is a passive kind of abuse. He is able to control you, and is especially distressing because you're suffering and the cause is not obvious.

Pity

You will be made to feel like you've suffered from his cheating spouse and abusive parents, untrustworthy boss, insane ex and on. He will try draw your feelings of compassion and stimulate your to nurture your instincts. Later on in the relationship should you make threats to leave He may inform you the end of his life is due to a serious illness such as cancer.

Triangulation

He forms a triangle that includes you and a third party like a parent, coworker or a mistress, and then pits both of them against one the other. The result is that he gets on the back foot and causes you to feel insecure about your relationship and want to hold onto your relationship. He wipes his hands clean while he observes you two in the middle of a conflict.

Gas lighting

The way in the narcissist deceives you into believing that you doubt your perception of things and your own sanity. He'll convince that you didn't see what you thought or heard something wrong, you didn't understand the situation, it wasn't in this manner and so on, until you question your own beliefs and trust everything that he says to you.

Projection

The man will cast all of his actions or emotions on your as if it were his. He will accuse you of being an opportunist because he's doing it in secret on you. He'll say that you're lying because he kept all the truth from you. It leaves you confused as well as defensive and broken.

Hoovering

Based on the vacuum cleaner's brand The fake narcissist's effort to lure you back in to him. He'll claim to be a different person or send you messages, inquire about your children and appear calm, then promise to see a therapist and so on. His goal is to returning his supply. He'll try for you to persuade you that everything can be different if you return.

Blaming and guilt

He will put blame onto you and make you feel guilt-ridden. He will claim that everything was your fault. You blamed yourself for everything. You didn't want to have sexual intimacy, you were an nagger, you lost weight, you complain too much about the man, placed your career ahead of it and other things. He'll convince you that he was bad because of you, and you caused him to take the risk. He could convince you that he is not lying and convince you to pay him for his supplies and again.

How to deal with the Narcissist

If you've come to the conclusion that there's someone who is a narcissist What do you do?

Take a moment to examine the situation.

Assess how serious this situation really is. Make an effort to learn about the background of the person who is narcissist and the degree of Narcissism. Recall or record what causes the narcissist to unleash narcissistic rage. Remember how he attempts to get you to do something about it. Pay attention to the methods employed by him. Be able to observe all of these actions objectively. Doing things that are influenced by emotion and crying just feed the Narcissist. The narcissist is already meticulously established a solid image or image and you may not be perceived as credible when you talk to people about it, so you need to be aware of your surroundings.

Accept the fact that the narcissist will not change.

We are hoping that you will be able knock mental apathy out of the narcissist or even explain the situation and help him won't succeed. In the event that the narcissist's concerns it is not his fault. wrong.

Ask for assistance.

Find counselors, friends or religious leaders parents- anyone who you can trust and can offer guidance and emotional help. They may also provide opinions from an objective perspective.

Set boundaries.

Note down the boundaries that the narcissist is not allowed to cross and the consequences in the event that they do. Note down your thoughts prior to speaking to the narcissist can make it easier to speak without sounding emotionally charged.

Be honest.

Recognize the limitations of the narcissist, and stay within the limitations. It's emotionally draining and a waste time to demand more from the narcissist that the person is capable of. Don't expect him be able to understand the importance of caring since he doesn't.

Keep in mind that the worth of an individual is not dependent on the person who is a narcissist.

Don't be a victim of getting involved with him. Instead, work on building confidence in yourself, meeting your needs, and following your passions.

Talk to them in a manner that makes them aware of the ways in which they can be benefited.

Instead of speaking up to say, plead, cry or screaming, take the time to change your language by focusing on what the person who is narcissistic will profit from it. It is important to learn how to draw attention to their self-centeredness. This is an effective strategy to be able to live in situations where you can't go away.

Present your ideas to the arrogant boss, if you have witnesses. When others listen to your ideas and discuss it, he'll find it difficult to give the credit.

Find evidence of or record any type of misuse.

Make use of technologies like CCTV and video recording for instance- to document the instances where abuse has occurred. Find witnesses who can support your claims.

Don't be fooled by the tactics of a narcissist and again.

Be aware of his strategies and keep yourself on guard against falling again for them. The narcissist might try to employ pity, projection, or hoovering. Be more shrewd this time. It could take time to master since you've developed a habit of being"the "Echo" and/or codependent. Being aware can assist you to stand up against.

Leave.

The best approach to dealing with a narcissist isn't to. To protect your physical and emotional well-being and your mental health It is recommended to get out. If you decide to leave expect a variety of strategies from the narcissist , either to cause your life to be miserable or get you (actually his food supply) back. There will be an emotional period similar to mourning after you depart. Find help and help to make it through this phase. Don't get too hard on yourself for allowing yourself to be deceived by a Narcissist. Your experience will make more shrewd, smarter and, eventually, ready for a positive relationship. While you're there, concentrate on your own needs and building confidence in yourself.

Chapter 12: All About Cognitive Dissonance

One aspect of the abusers is that they employ cognitive dissonance to establish control. In this article, we'll explain the nature of this, what it has to do with gaslighting, as well as what you can do to stop it.

Usually, this phrase is used to describe the emotions and discomfort that arise when your beliefs do not align with the ideas of others or there's no information provided to you. In most cases, the aim of this is to ensure consistency with regards to beliefs and opinions which is why when beliefs that you consider to be true are questioned, or what you do doesn't match with what others believe, some people make sure that dissonance is minimized or changed in order to change it more palatable so that the issue doesn't exist any longer a problem.

It may seem like an excellent thing however it's not. The most popular method of describing it is, of course "explaining things out." This is what you see frequently with abusers and there's an explanation for why this is the primary goal of abusers.

What's the Origin Of This

The concept was first suggested by a psychologist called Leon Festinger, who first came up with this idea because it's an idea that people apply to ensure that their beliefs are consistent. This is due to the fact that they want to keep their actions and beliefs that are a part of them.

The reason for what is being said is the idea of harmony. If there is a conflict in opinions or even concepts that cause conflict, it can lead to discord. It's an inherent way to avoid conflict, and instead, to promote harmony in your life.

Festinger later published a book titled A Theory of Cognitive Dissonance that was published in the year 1957. The concept behind this book was that this is an annexed state that will eventually lead to an improvement in dissonance. They'll engage in an activity to decrease the dissonance taking place. This is a completely different mindset than what other people have to deal with, but it's a powerful one. It's affected by other elements also.

The Power Of The Dissonance

Dissonance can be a bit different for everyone This is something you'll be able to understand from the beginning. It's based on certain aspects which are essential. Here are the elements which usually determine the cognitive dissonance of something, and the reason why it is important.

* Thoughts that are based on more of a personal meaning to them are more dissonant including your self-beliefs

* The dissonance ratio is determined by the clash of and harmonious or consonant thoughts. You try to achieve perfect harmony, no matter the situation.

* The beliefs you believe in that are held more often create a greater dissonance

• The greater dissonance you feel, the greater pressure is placed on you to feel that discomfort.

The most amazing thing about this is that cognitive dissonance can be an issue that can be seen throughout the spectrum of our lives. Typically it is evident when there's the conflict of opinions And often you don't even recognize it's happening until it's too late.

Let's look at this situation You want to be more eco-friendly and you purchase an SUV that gets poor gas mileage.

It's your idea that you would like to reduce emissions, however the problem with driving a vehicle that's not good for the environment, maybe because you think it'll help get your children to practice soccer better is on the front.

This is also the case when you hear people claim that they're against materialistic values, and then decide to buy an extra house.

The dissonance can be resolved in two ways. It is possible to sell the car in order to buy a more environmentally sustainable vehicle, or the individual is a minimalist and then gets smaller accommodation to live in, and promotes the practice of minimalism in their families.

You can also choose the third option that allows them to reduce the discomfort they feel when they have an environmental responsibility. Sometimes, they'll argue it out, explaining their own rationale or they might opt to use public transportation or ride their bicycle whenever they can or attempt to walk everywhere. Perhaps the solution to make the home more sustainable is figuring out better ways to use the home to lessen the environmental impact of the house.

This theory basically suggests that people will keep doing what they are doing, even if it's harmful to them.

This is a common sight and especially among those who smoke.

Smoking cigarettes is extremely harmful, and it could lead to deaths in a lot of instances However, there are some who realize that they may be dead if they continue to smoke but continue to smoke.

Why do they think that way? They believe that they'll either think that it's worth the health disadvantages. Another way to approach reduce these negative effects. Smokers will, from that point on convince themselves that even if they continue smoking cigarettes, they'll not gain weight If they decide to quit smoking, they'll eventually in gaining weight, even though they realize that they do this method to deal by not having to gain weight.

Another excellent example is when a smoker states "yeah I'm aware that it's not good for my health, yet I experience more anxiety, and this helps me calm to sleep." The smokers are very skilled in explaining dissonance.

If you know someone is an alcohol user but is unable to make the change. They'll either stop completely and attempt to do so or try to justify their behavior by the argument that "if I do not drink, I'll suffer terrible headaches and it helps keep my thoughts under control." But is it reallywork?

You're not solving the issue. It's like applying one of the tiny band-aids to the wound that is causing it to get worse. You may think that it's helping however in reality it's actually hurting you more than it is helping.

How Does This Affect Gaslighting?

In simple terms cognitive dissonance is yet another technique used by the narcissistic abusers. This is due to the fact that it is utilized by those who abuse narcissists frequently, and is often the result of gaslighting, in a way.

This is the place where they cause confusion, disbelief and a belief that it isn't possible to be just like the other people.

Cognitive dissonance does not always occur when you are abused. Some people might think that gaslighting is a separate issue however it's something that occurs since a lot of times, narcissists make use of this as a type of snap.

In the case of gaslighting, there are more subtle ways to do this and more barbs in a comment on what people do, however it is possible to find cognitive dissonance with certain forms of gaslighting.

Let's look at an illustration. There is the person who abuses, who is attracted to someone they are able to manipulate, and will instantly declare their lovefor the person, claiming they're "fate" and will even reach the point that they'd like to have a wedding date set in stone.

The lover begins to be drawn to it and ends getting in love with the person, but they do not realize that the victim has a motive behind it. The spouse has a dream wedding in mind and believes that this is the way it will happen and that they'll get this dream wedding with everything perfect.

Of course, it's not.

In the midst of the wedding, or when the spouse begins to discuss their marriage and the person who is being abused alters their position by saying that they don't want to be married, and that they believe it's ridiculous.

They then begin to smirk, saying that the person who is "crazy" to think they'll ever marry They will then begin attacking those who believe they would like to be married. One who is averse to the notion of marriage doubts what they'd like to do in the present and then blame falls on the other person. Since they're definitely "rushing" things into the relationship.

The funny thing is that the person who was abused did the deciding and wanted it. The spouse remembers that the abuser discussed the future and even getting married.

The abuser was manipulating the victim and wanted control and control over the other person. And they'll be in a disagreement of opinions.

The person who is abused doesn't want to be married, but the partner comes up with you agreed with this and the abuser is faced with a dilemma. Instead of being accountable for the actions that he's committed, and possibly finding a compromise to lessen the conflict or dissonance, he minimizes the dissonance through, naturally, gazing at and disproving the claim of the partner.

Cognitive dissonance and gaslighting are two sides of the same coin, however it is possible to say it's a method by which the victim explains his actions and explains the reason why he is able to continue with the other partner. However, the cognitive dissonance doesn't only focused on the person who is being abused and the partner, but also on the person who believes they're going to be married. This creates confusion, and an unhindered reality for all. This leaves the person in a state of confusion with a flurry of emotion and hurt being aware that the beliefs they believed in were smashed to the ground, and can make them feel like they've been let down.

However, the one who was in a gaslight state begins to think if they are not in the right, or they were the villain and if they're thinking about this. In the end, there's a reason why couples get married so quickly would they not?

This is a tactic that for those who have suffered abuse. have experienced, and they believe that they are the only ones with an idea, only to see it completely shattered later on.

A Few More Examples

Let's go over some additional examples will we?

Let's examine how gaslighting is closely linked with cognitive dissonance.

You can see it in the film from 1944 named Gaslight Which happened for the principal character. She believed something, however her abuser said a different thing. This is what will cause the victim to doubt what they are experiencing , and the person being hurt also. The perpetrator will continue to do this, to make people doubt their own experience, and then, use the power and control they will gain from this.

It's certainly in the interest of the individual's wellbeing.

Another instance is from the film Sleeping with the Enemy which was released in 1991. In the movie the victim was a stalker and would often be found at her house, straightening the bath towels from time to time and often. She knew that her lover was meticulous about cleanliness and when she thinks that she's alone, she discovers that she's not. This is something the victim will do to frighten the principal character. In this case, it led to the person be verbally assaulted every when she would notice this, then make a make a comment about it and then be ripped down.

However, you can see this all over the place. At work there are times when you perform something, and obviously, the coworker who is narcissistic will claim that you aren't doing anything, and will often do this in order to cause confusion the other personsince, they're "clearly not performing their duties" which is only going to get more difficult from now on. The person being the victim of this is, naturally totally confused since they believe that they're doing what's right however they're not, and it's only going to get worse each attempt to disprove it as they'll usually be demolished again.

How to Distinguish This?

What can you do to diffuse this yet again? It is a matter of by the person who is in the midst of the narcissists' abuse and gaslighting receives the affirmation and validation.

Validation is among the most crucial aspects for those who have suffered from gaslighting or narcissists' abuse. This is due to the fact that it will make them feel that their words are true, and the events they endured actually took place.

If they don't be validated, they are confused about what's happening The gaslighting can make people feel that their memories aren't correct. With validation it will begin to ease this.

If you're in and have overcame the gaslighting and abuse taking a trip to the therapist and sharing your personal issuesor journaling can be beneficial.

For those who are in a situation that they aren't yet leaving I suggest journaling, but in a manner that the other person isn't able to find it.

But, it's not the only thing you'll need to accomplish because narcissistic abuse is likely to persist to haunt you if you don't take care and it's best to begin to overcome the trauma related to this, particularly when you have an unconditional, positive and positive validation being offered. This is a fantastic approach to help you heal from the pain and help you feel more confident about your recovery. It is possible to feel confident once you overcome the grief and trauma, and the ability to speak about your experience is an excellent way for the person who has survived to reduce the cognitive dissonance to proceed to healing. Talking to someone can help however, you have to decide to do it.

We'll go over a little more about ways to be helped by the abuse in the next chapter as well as discuss some strategies you can employ to assist to escape the abuse.

Cognitive dissonance is a frequent problem that can be experienced when you are dealing with narcissistic abuse and this chapter outlined the causes, as well as why it is crucial to address this issue.

Chapter 13: Techniques Of Gaslighting

Do You Really Want to

Gaslighters are a regular and pathological liar. They will openly lie to you and will not stop or change their story even when they are called out or prove their deceit. The principle of lying is their destructive behaviour. Even if you are aware that they lie they are able to be convincing. At the end of the day you start doubting your own judgment.

Do Not Discredit You to Others

The gaslighter spreads gossip and rumors about you to the public. They might appear to be concerned about your behavior and "your behaviour" while subtly stating to people that you are insane or unstable. This tactic could be very effective, and a lot of people could be influenced by the bully or abuser without understanding the whole situation. In addition, the gaslighter could lie to you , telling people that they are insane. Remember that people who don't know you might not say a negative one about you however the gaslighter will try everything to convince you that they will.

Deflect the topic at hand

If you ask a gaslighter questions or if you make a complaint for something they said or did or said, they could shift the conversation with a question instead of addressing the issue in question. They might blatantly deny the circumstances by saying things similar to: "You're making things up. This has never happened."

Take a step back from your thoughts and feelings.

Through minimizing your thoughts and feelings the gaslighter can take control of you. They could make statements such as: "Calm down," "You're reacting too much," or "Why are you so sensitive?" These statements reduce what you're feeling or what you're thinking and signal that you're wrong. If you have to deal with those who do not acknowledge your thoughts, opinions or feelings and feelings, you'll begin to doubt them. In addition, you don't feel understood or validated which is a huge challenge to manage.

Shift blame to You

Blame-shifting is a technique used by gaslighters. Every conversation is in some way twisted so that you're the culprit for an incident that occurred. Even when you discuss the impact their actions have on how you feel, they can manage to alter the conversation to ultimately blame you. That is, they alter the circumstances so that you believe that you're the reason of their behaviour. They say that if you had behaved differently, they wouldn't behave the way they do.

Deny Any Wrongdoing

The notoriously abusive and bullies are known for their refusal to admit they committed any wrong. They do this to avoid the blame for their bad choices. It also causes the victim to be in a state of confusion and frustration as there is no acknowledgement of the hurt they caused.

This also makes it difficult for the victim to get over or heal from the abuse or bullying.

Use words of compassion to use as a weapon

When confronted or asked questions the gaslighter may use sweet and loving phrases in an attempt to soften the issue. For instance they could use phrases like "You already know that I cherish you. I'd never harm you intentionally." The words and the apology are the ones you would like to be hearing, but they're not genuine, particularly in the event that the same act repeats itself over and over.

If you're dealing somebody who is using gaslighting to manipulate others You must be attentive to the actions of the person, not to words.

Reframe and Twist Conversations

The majority of the time, this tactic is employed when you're discussing something that has happened within the last. For example the case where your friend shoved your body against the wall, and you then discuss the incident later, they could modify the incident to their advantage. They might claim that he did not really push you but rather that you ran away from him, and that he tried to hold you, and caused you to fall to the wall. If stories and experiences are constantly repeated to his advantage it is possible to doubt your own version of events and that is precisely the goal.

Chapter 14: Languages Narcissists Usually Use to smear you.

The following list includes more than a hundred of the things Narcissists are known to say. Make careful to watch out for certain things that you might have heard someone tell you. If you're not certain if you're having a conversation with someone who is a narcissist not, this list can help you determine if you're having a conversation with one not.

If you are able to make a statement that someone else has previously or is telling you about it constantly and you don't know why, it's an indication that you're dealing with someone who is a person who is a narcissist. All of these compilations are genuine compilations that were allegedly told by Narcissists telling their victims.

You're irrational. You need to get checked for schizophrenia or bipolar.

You're always inventing all sorts of things in your head.

Professional help is required. I'm not averse to doing the wrong thing.

Why do you feel so defensive? You're too young . You have to learn to speak more clearly.

I'm not fighting with you, I'm discussing things with you. It's not my intention to say that you should be different. I'm not trying to convince anyone that there's always something wrong in you. You're one weird freak. Whatever!!. If you weren't angry with me off, I would not have sent those nasty messages to you. Everyone has an issue with you. If you talk to them about me, they will do _____ and harm you, (They will either making up exaggerated claims to get back at them or even blackmail you to expose them). I was once convinced you were a nice person (because you're now down to their level and shoving the truth).

What is it that makes you such a jerk? you need to get over it. I am already late. I was supposed to be here by noon, but now it's 2:40 p.m. Are you really would like to go out? Or not. I'm not interested in your games of wits. You can just forget them about me and I'll cause your life to be a living hell. They're very adept at calling you names , quite shocking names which you don't hear from anyone else. I'm smarter than you dumb ass. You can try it, and then you'll lose to me. I'm likely to kiss them on the back and then we'll discuss the person they'd like to have in their lives (It's like two people competing). You'd think they'd have figured this out by now. You cannot beat me. You must take yourself to the ground to make fools of yourself.

If you're making a call before an audience, they'll inform you that you require help so that they won't be able to play anymore. They'll say something like, "I feel really sorry for you, I'm going to leave, and because I don't want forced into another argument. On the other hand, could say, "I don't know what you're talking about or what are you talking about," then turn off his phone and then contact you to say that something along the lines of "bitch Have you discovered that you aren't going to beat me." They're just trying to make you think they're crazy by trying to convince other people on their side that you're crazy and crazy.

They'll say something like, you're totally insane and I'm not convinced that I am being forced to do this. When they finally leave the phone they laugh and moan and tell everyone what a jerk you are. They'll say "what do you mean by I don't have any friends, there is an attorney friend , and that attorney friend has a lot of friends, you're the depressed person who is at home, and you do not make any new friends. I'm so sorry you're the only pet rescue companion, wow". "I did not realize that you are more noble than you think. You are victimized, and that's why I avoid, Poor you! You're wondering why I keep clear of you".

Others think I'm a nice person however I aren't. I'll stay away from you for as long as you keep putting me down. It's no wonder I'm talking about drug! If I desire to feel like a shit all I have to do is be near you. What's doing for you? Listen to what you're saying. Are you an unlucky loser?

If they decide to leave and take a nice ride and tolerate the rest of you, they will tell you something like "oh she's fine with eating breakfast in bed, and we will be going to Hawaii. You could have lived the most perfect life that you could have ever had however, you decided to fight me every single time". We'll talk about it when I'm millionaire. My Facebook friends, who have never had a chance to meet in person always compliment me on how clever I am. I'm not trying to influence you. are the one considering your former husband. And you're making fun of me. There is always a problem. I am the most wonderful thing that's been happening to you. No one else will have the same love for you as I do.

It's always your responsibility. What is the reason you become angry and bitter about every single thing? You're always searching for something to discuss all the time. What can you do to stay clear of being a mood every day? I'm sure that's enjoyable for you. I believe I'm the only person who truly likes you. Nobody else does. It's impossible to manage me, you bitch. I'm not concerned about your children.

Everyone agrees that you're a horrible person! You're insane mad! You're lazy!

You're too sensitive. I can hear your thoughts. You're not a listener to anyone. I'll reimburse you. It's time to wash your face, or I'll pay you back. You're just a piece rubbish and a shit. If you attempt to alert them to an act they committed and they're likely to be in trouble legally, they'll say that something along the lines of "shut in, what a smug oddo." You're worried about everything and have done this before. Therefore, they will always try to prove they know more than you do, by telling people what they think about you.

After cheating repeatedly on you He tries to claim that you were the one have said nice things to him. There's no other man as nice as me. If he's out with someone, they will inform you that they had fun since I'm there. I'm an Canadian bloodline, which means naturally, I'm more intelligent than you. My work is more important, while you are just working on your assignments. You sit and play on the computer all day long. I didn't get back to you on your text because you continue to annoy me with your stupidity. They are now doing this in order to cause you to feel like a child , and to make you feel you're not enough.

This is my route or highway. Women are here to help men. If you're so good in budgeting, then why aren't we in a better position? (That is after having lost his money at a gambling establishment) I am able to handle _____. I know the reason why _____. I have the solution to everything. You only need to be listening to me _____. I know the solutions to all questions. I am aware of the motives of people. I have the answers to parenting. I know the reason as to the reason your child ran off at you. He says He has all the answers and would like to get you to take note of him.

In the days when I was living in Florida I was wealthy I was familiar with all the film stars because I grew up with them. I didn't have to be worried about breaking constantly. He may have been in Florida and was familiar with all the film Stars however this did not stop him from becoming financially broke.

What do I think I'll do next? I raced Porsches in the Indy 500 and I had two burgers King's along with pizza dough rolls. No wonder your daughter can't maintain her boyfriend. She's just like you. (Now he's telling you since he's aware that every mother will be adamant about her kids and, when someone attacks your children, you are angry, you will respond).

The majority of Narcissist is prone to this behavior when he claims that you're getting cracking his ear and winning. He will then begin to pull out every shit that makes you feel sensitive. They'll start pointing off the idea that you have had a negative relations with your boss or someone close to you. They may compare you with that person. If you have a great relationship with someone they might tell you to them to tear you down in the event that they are unable to get revenge. They will do whatever to make you feel uncomfortable and make you feel bad. They will say that something similar to that is true. He'll say, "I know at least three people in this community who believe you're insane and mentally ill. They'll always accuse you of being crazy or bipolar since they're the tactic to make you appear insane.

There are times when you begin to believe you're truly insane, particularly if you have been doing you've had it for quite a while. People will believe that you're crazy. Additionally, he's incredibly lavish. He will attempt to exaggerate his accomplishments, and is constantly talking about people know him. He wants you to think of you are a genius and will speak in your face.

For an Narcissist it is impossible to find anything beneficial to them, not even them. This is why they're so judgmental of all things and everyone else around them. They'll say something such as, "you just want to revisit your past." This past is might be the past from yesterday. They might say that you ought to have known that it was not the right moment to contact me or to call me via phone. Then they'll be followed by a justified anger that you treat me like a fool and aren't taking drugs. Nobody likes you. They'll try to make fun at you when they slap you on the phone. They'll tell you something like, "You wanted to know if I'm okay.

There's always something wrong in you. If you quit me, you'll end up tattooed and blue! You'll never have confidence enough to let me go. You are be delusional. There are no people who like you. You're not liked by anyone and you're too old. You will never be liked by anyone. You're overweight Nobody will ever truly love you like me. There is no one who is as great as I am. There is no one who will be as patient with your needs and leave like I do. You'll never get the same house as mine. It is likely that you will live in a car that is broken located on the north side.

I am all you need. Do you think you'll ever have enough food to sustain yourself? I didn't realize that you're so crazy. You're in need of a shrink. I've never done that. You are just insane. I'm able to say or do whatever I want to say to you because I'm looking for you to. I was busy, and everyone must earn an income. I worked hard but no one seems to be concerned about it. Nobody is going to be as passionate about you as I am Why do you constantly be a critic I'm not a nag and why do you constantly get me offended? I'm just laughing at you.

I would like to _____. I require me me. What is rage? Can't I be angry?

Only I can treat you as a shite. (This is a phrase woman narcissists may declare, even though she does not speak it in the exact phrases. She may say it because she is her property, however, she won't say it because she is in love with you. I didn't say anything to you because I believed that you were aware of her feelings about you. She was constantly bringing up your name and I wasn't sure if that you two were close. They continue to use the world as a reason to talk about you.

They'll discover that You have gorgeous blue eyes, and when you say "oh thank you!" They'll say that something along the lines of "I cannot do it any more." If you ask if you are breakup with me once more and they'll say yes. (So they will tell you that they are amazing, and at the same time, they break up with you).

The next two words are ones you should take seriously. If you ever commit a crime against me and I find out, I'll kill the person who did it and also end up killing you. (So If this person threatens you with death or has any reason to think there's reasons to be concerned trying to get out of the situation). The whole thing started when you initiated it. (This is an indication of an argument you didn't begin). Grow up and get over it.

Conclusion

Avoiding the contact of gaslighters can be one the most effective ways to free yourself from being gaslighted. But, it isn't an option in all cases like co-parenting. It is essential to set healthy boundaries, get help, and seek the advice of the mental health and legal professionals to obtain additional help in situations that you are unable to escape the gaslighter. If you are employed by or working with a gaslighter be aware that if you feel threatened you, there are laws in place to protect the situation.

Gaslighters, not just in your home, but also at the international and national scale can have a great deal of influence. You've witnessed how gaslighters are easily transformed into dictators and cult leader which makes it impossible to comprehend the facts and the flimsy reality. Being able to identify people who are not in agreement is the main problem for leaders of gaslighting. So, be as informed as you can about the current news and gaslighting. If a report on news is not straight or accurate generally, it's. The practice of gaslighting is often propagated in the press. Being a responsible citizen it is your right voice your opinion, and make your voice heard through casting a vote.

There's every opportunity to improve your life better, no matter the amount of gaslighting you're subjected to. It is possible to have hope that is always there. It can be difficult initially to implement positive changes like abstaining from those who light up the road, setting limits and avoiding talking to strangers but it's worth the rewards of greater tranquility, happier children and better health.

www.ingramcontent.com/pod-product-compliance
Lightning Source LLC
Chambersburg PA
CBHW060333030426
42336CB00011B/1322